The Prodigious Hickey: A Lawrenceville Story

Owen Johnson

THE PRODIGIOUS HICKEY

First Published as "The Eternal Boy"

CALIFORNIA

" Hickey it was . . . who . . . organised the
midnight feasts "

The Prodigious Hickey

A LAWRENCEVILLE STORY

By OWEN JOHNSON

Author of "The Varmint," "The Humming Bird," "Max Fargus," etc.

ILLUSTRATED

A. L. BURT COMPANY

Publishers   *New York*

CONTENTS

THE AWAKENING OF HICKEY

" ' He forged a thunderbolt and hurled it at what? At the proudest blood in Europe, the Spaniard, and sent him home conquered; at the most warlike blood in Europe, the French ' " . . .

Shrimp Davis, on the platform, piped forth the familiar periods of Phillips's oration on Toussaint L'Ouverture, while the Third Form in declamation, disposed to sleep, stirred fitfully on one another's shoulders, resenting the adolescent squeak that rendered perfect rest impossible. Pa Dater followed from the last bench, marking the position of the heels, the adjustment of the gesture to the phrase,

and the rise and fall of the voice with patient enthusiasm, undismayed by the memory of the thousand Toussaints who had passed, or the certainty of
the thousands who were to come.

"I would call him Napoleon, but Napoleon made
his way to empire over broken oaths and through a
sea of BLOOD," shrieked the diminutive orator with
a sudden crescendo as a spitball, artfully thrown,
sung by his nose.

At this sudden shrill notice of approaching man-
hood, Hickey, in the front row, roused himself with
a jerk, put both fists in his eyes and glanced with
indignant reproach at the embattled disturber of
his privileges. Rest now being impossible, he decided to revenge himself by putting forth a series
of faces as a sort of running illustration to the
swelling cadences. Shrimp Davis struggled man-
fully to keep his eyes from the antics of his tormentor. He accosted the ceiling, he looked sadly on
the floor. He gazed east and west profoundly,
through the open windows, seeking forgetfulness in
the distant vistas. All to no purpose. Turn where
he might the mocking face of Hickey danced after
him. At the height of his eloquence Shrimp choked,
clutched at his mouth, exploded into laughter and

tumbled ingloriously to his seat amid the delighted shrieks of the class.

Pa Dater, surprised and puzzled, rose with solemnity and examined the benches for the cause of the outbreak. Then taking up a position on the platform, from which he could command each face, he scanned the roll thoughtfully and announced, " William Orville Hicks."

Utterly unprepared and off his guard, Hickey drew up slowly to his feet. Then a flash of inspiration came to him.

" Please, Mr. Dater," he said with simulated regret, " I chose the same piece."

Delighted, he settled down, confident that the fortunate coincidence would at least postpone his appearance.

" Indeed," said Mr. Dater with a merciless smile, " isn't that extraordinary! Well, Hicks, try and lend it a new charm."

Hickey hesitated with a calculating glance at the already snickering class. Then forced to carry through the bravado, he climbed over the legs of his seat-mates and up to the platform, made Mr. Dater a deep bow, and gave the class a quick bob of his head, accompanied by a confidential wink from that eye which happened to be out of the master's scrutiny. He glanced down, shook the wrinkles from his trousers, buttoned his coat, shot his cuffs and assumed the recognised Websterian attitude. Twice he cleared his throat while the class waited expectantly for the eloquence that did not surge. Next he frowned, took one step forward and two back, sunk his hands in his trousers and searched for the missing sentences on the moulding that ran around the edge of the ceiling.

"Well, Hicks, what's wrong?" said the master with difficult seriousness. "Haven't learned it?"

"Oh, yes, sir," said Hickey with dignity.

"What's the matter then?"

"Please, sir," said Hickey, with innocent frankness, "I'm afraid I'm a little embarrassed."

The class guffawed loud and long. The idea of Hickey succumbing to such an emotion was irresistible. Shrimp Davis sobbed hysterically and gratefully.

Hickey alone remained solemn, grieved and misunderstood.

"Well, Hicks," continued the master with the ghost of a smile, "embarrassment is something that you should try to overcome."

At this Turkey Reiter led Shrimp Davis out in agony.

"Very well," said Hickey with an injured look, "I'll try, sir. I'll do my best. But I don't think the conditions are favourable."

Mr. Dater commanded silence. Hickey bowed again and raised his head cloaked in seriousness. A titter acclaimed him. He stopped and looked appealingly at the master.

"Go on, Hicks, go on," said Mr. Dater. "Do your best. At least, let us hear the words."

Another inspiration came to Hickey. "I don't think that this is quite regular, sir," he said aggressively. "I have always taken an interest in my work, and I don't see why I should be made to sacrifice a good mark."

Mr. Dater bit his lips and quieted the storm with two upraised fingers.

"Nevertheless, Hicks," he said, "I think we shall allow you to continue."

"What!" exclaimed Hickey as though loath to credit his ears. Then adding calm to dignity, he said, "Very well, sir,—not prepared!"

With the limp of a martyr, he turned his back on Mr. Dater, and returned to his seat, where he sat in injured dignity, disdaining to notice the grimaces of his companions.

Class over, the master summoned Hicks, and bent his brows, boring him with a look of inquisitorial accusation.

" Hicks," he said, spacing his words, " I have felt, for the last two weeks, a certain lack of discipline here. Just a word to the wise, Hicks, just a word to *the wise!* "

Hickey was pained. Where was the evidence to warrant such a flat accusation? He had been arraigned on suspicion, that was all, absolutely on mere haphazard suspicion. And this was justice?

Moreover, Hickey's sensitive nature was shocked. He had always looked upon Pa Dater as an antagonist for whose sense of fair play he would have answered as for his own. And now to be accused thus with innuendo and veiled menace—then he could have faith in no master, not one in the whole faculty! And this grieved Hickey mightily as he went moodily along the halls.

Now, the code of a schoolboy's ethics is a marvellously fashioned thing—and by that each master stands or falls. To be accused of an offence of which he is innocent means nothing, for it simply demon-

strates the lower calibre of the master's intelligence.
But to be suspected and accused on mere suspicion
of something which he has just committed,—that
is unpardonable, and in absolute violation of the
laws of warfare, which decree that the struggle shall
be one of wits, without recourse to the methods of
the inquisition.

Hickey, disillusionised and shocked, went glumly
down the brownstone steps of Memorial and slowly
about the green circle, resisting the shouted invita-
tions to tarry under the nourishing apple trees.

He felt in him an imperative need to strike back,
to instantly break some rule of the tyranny that en-
compassed him. With this heroic intention he walked
nonchalantly up the main street to the jigger-shop,
which no underformer may enter until after four. As
he approached the forbidden haunt, suddenly the
figure of Mr. Lorenzo Blackstone Tapping, the young
assistant housemaster at the Dickinson, more popu-
larly known as "Tabby," rolled up on a bicycle.

"Humph, Hicks!" said at once Mr. Tapping
with a suspicious glance at the jigger-shop directly
opposite, "how do you happen to be here out of
hours?"

"Please, sir," said Hickey glibly, "I've got a

nail that's sticking into my foot. I was just going to Bill Orum's to get it fixed."

"Humph!" Mr. Tapping gave him a searching look, hesitated and mounting his wheel continued, unconvinced.

"He looked back," said Hickey wrathfully, peering through the misty windows of the cobbler's shop. Then smarting at the injury, he added, "He didn't believe me—the sneak!"

It was a second reminder of the tyranny he lived under. He waited a moment, found the coast clear and flashed across to the jigger-shop. Half drugstore, half confectioner's, the jigger-shop was the property of Doctor Furnell, whose chief interest in life consisted in a devotion to the theory of the millennium, to the lengthy expounding of which an impoverished boy would sometimes listen in the vain hope of establishing a larger credit. On every-day occasions the shop was under the charge of "Al," a creature without heart or pity, who knew the exact financial status of each of the four hundred odd boys, even to the amount and date of his allowance. Al made no errors, his sympathies were deaf to the call, and he never (like the doctor), committed the mistake of returning too much change.

Al welcomed him with a grunt, carefully closing the little glass doors that protected the tray of éclairs and fruit cake, and leaning back drawled:

"What's the matter, Hickey? You look kind of discouraged."

"Give me a coffee jigger, with a chocolate syrup and a dash of whipped cream—stick a meringue in it," said Hickey. Then as Al remained passively expectant, he drew out a coin, saying, "Oh, I've got the money!"

He ate gloomily and, in silence, refusing to be drawn into conversation. Something was wrong in the scheme of things. Twice in the same hour he had been regarded with suspicion and an accusing glance,—his simplest explanation discountenanced! Up to this time, he had been like a hundred other growing boys, loving mischief for mischief's sake, entering into a lark with no more definite purpose than the zest of an adventure. Of course he regarded a master as the Natural Enemy, but he had viewed him with the tolerance of an agile monkey for a wolf who does not climb. Now slowly it began to dawn upon him that there was an ethical side.

He vanished suddenly behind the counter as Mr. Tapping, returning, made directly for the jigger-shop. Hickey, at the end of the long counter, crouching amid stationery, heard him moving suspiciously toward his hiding place. Quickly he flicked a pencil down behind the counter and vanished through the back entrance as Tapping, falling into the trap, sprang in the direction of the noise.

The adventure served two purposes: it gave Hickey the measure of the enemy, and it revealed to him where first to strike.

II

The President of the Dickinson by virtue of the necessary authority to suppress all insubordination was Turkey Reiter, broad of shoulder, speckled and battling of face, but the spirit of the Dickinson was Hickey. Hickey it was, lank of figure and keen of feature, bustling of gait and drawling of speech, with face as innocent as a choir-boy's, who planned the revolts against the masters, organised the midnight feasts and the painting of water-towers. His genius lived in the nicknames of the Egg-head, Beauty Sawtelle, Morning Glory, Red Dog, Wash Simmons and the Coffee Cooler, which he had bestowed on his comrades with unfailing felicity.

Great was Hickey, and Macnooder was his pro-

phet. Doc Macnooder roomed just across the hall. He was a sort of genius of all trades. He played quarter on the eleven and ran the half mile close to the two-minute mark. He was the mainstay of Banjo, Mandolin and Glee Clubs. He played the organ in chapel and had composed the famous Hamill House March in memory of his requested departure from that abode. He organised the school dramatic club. He was secretary and treasurer of his class and of every organisation to which he belonged. He received a commission from a dozen firms to sell to his likenesses, stationery, athletic goods, choice sets of books, fin de siecle neckties, fancy waistcoats, fountain pens and safety razors, all of which articles, if report is to be credited, he sold with ease and eloquence at ten per cent. above the retail price. His room was a combination of a sorcerer's den and junk-shop. At one corner a row of shelves held a villainous array of ill-smelling black, green and blue bottles, with which he was prepared to instantly cure anything from lockjaw to snake bite.

The full measure of Macnooder's activities was never known. Turkey Reiter had even surprised him drawing up a will for Bill Orum, the cobbler, to whom he had just sold a cure for rheumatism.

It was to Macnooder that Hickey opened his
heart and his need of vengeance. It cannot be said
that the ethical side of the struggle appealed to
Macnooder, who had small predilection for phi-
losophy and none at all for the moral sciences, but
the love of mischief was strong. The encounter with
Tapping in the morning had suggested a victim near
at hand and conveniently inexperienced.

Mr. Tapping in advance of young Mr. Baldwin (of whom it shall be related) had arrived at
Lawrenceville the previous year with latter-day
theories on the education of boys. As luck would
have it, Mr. Rogers, the housemaster, would be absent that evening at a little dinner of old classmates
in Princeton, leaving the entire conduct of the Dickinson in the hands of his assistant. In passing, it
must be noted that between the two masters there
was little sympathy. Mr. Rogers had lived too long
in the lair of the boy to be at all impressed with the
new ideas on education that Mr. Tapping and later
Mr. Baldwin advocated in the blissful state of their
ignorance.

At three o'clock, Tapping departed to convey to
a class of impatient boys, decked out in athletic
costumes with base-balls stuffed in their pockets and

tennis rackets waiting at their sides, the interesting shades of distinction in that exciting study, Greek prose composition.   Then Hickey gleefully, while Macnooder guarded the stairs, entered the study, and with a screw-driver loosened the screw which held the inner door-knob, to the extent that it could later be easily removed with the fingers.

At half past seven o'clock, when study hour had begun, Hickey entered the sanctum ostensibly for advice on a perplexing problem in advanced algebra.

Mr. Tapping did not like Hickey.   He regarded him with suspicion, with an instinctive recognition of an enemy.   Also he was engaged in the difficult expression of a certain letter which, at that time, presented more difficulties than the binomial theorem. So he inquired with short cordiality, concealing the written page under a blotter:

" Well, Hicks, what is it? "

" Please, Mr. Tapping," said Hickey, who had perceived the move with malignant delight, " I wish you'd look at this problem,—it won't work out." He added (shades of a thousand boys!), " I think there must be some mistake in the book."

Now, the chief miseries of a young assistant master centre about the study hours; when theory demands that he should be ready to advise and instruct the discouraged boyish mind on any subject figuring in the curriculum, whatever be his preference or his prejudice. Mr. Tapping, who romped over the Greek and Latin page, had an hereditary weakness in the mathematics, a failing that the boys had discovered and instantly turned to their profit. He took the book, glanced at the problem and began to jot down a line of figures. Hickey, meanwhile, with his back to the door, brazenly extracted the loosened screw.

Finally, Mr. Tapping, becoming hopelessly entangled, raised his head and said with a disdainful smile: "Hicks, I think you had better put a little work on this—just a little work!"

"Mr. Tapping, I don't understand it," said Hickey, adding to himself, "Old Tabby is up a tree!"

"Nonsense—perfectly easy, perfectly simple," said Tapping, returning the book with a gesture of dismissal, "requires a little application, Hicks, just a little application—that's all."

Hickey, putting on his most injured look, bowed to injustice and departed at the moment that Turkey Reiter entered, seeking assistance in French. Upon his tracks, without an interval, succeeded Macnooder with a German composition, Hungry Smeed to discuss history, the Egghead on a question of spelling, and Beauty Sawtelle in thirst for information about the Middle Ages. Finally, Mr. Tapping's patience, according to Macnooder's prophetic calculation, burst on a question of biblical interpretation, and announcing wrathfully that he could no longer be disturbed, he ushered out the last tormentor and shut the door with violence.

Presently Hickey stole up on tiptoe and fastening a noose over the knob, gave a signal. The string, pulled by a dozen equally responsible hands, carried away the knob, which fell with a tiny crash and spun in crazy circles on the floor. The fall of the inner useless knob was heard on the inside of the door and the exclamation that burst from the startled master. The tyrant was caged,—the house was at their pleasure!

Mr. Tapping committed the initial mistake of knocking twice imperiously on the door and commanding, "Open at once."

Two knocks answered him. Then he struck three violent blows and three violent echoes returned, while a bunch of wriggling, chuckling boys clustered at every crack of the door, listening with strained ears for the muffled roars that came from within.

While one group began a game of leap-frog, another, under the guidance of Hickey, descended into the housemaster's quarters and proceeded to attend to the rearrangement of the various rooms. Working beaver-like with whispered cautions, they rapidly exchanged the furniture of the parlour with the dining-room, grouping each transformed room, exactly as the original had been.

Then they placed the six-foot water-cooler directly in front of the entrance with a tin pan balanced, to give the alarm, and shaking with silent expectant laughter extinguished all lights, undressed and returned to the corridors, white, shadowy forms, to wait developments. Meanwhile, the caged assistant master continued to pound upon the door with a fury that betokened a state of approaching hysteria.

At half past ten, suddenly the tin pan crashed horribly on the floor. A second later every boy was sleeping loudly in his bed. Astonished at such a reception, Mr. Rogers groped into the darkness and fell against the water-cooler, which in his excitement he embraced and carried over with him to the floor. Recovering himself, he lighted the gas and perceived the transformed parlour and dining-room. Then he started for the assistant housemaster's rooms, with long, angry bounds, saying incoherent, expressive things to himself.

The ordeal that young Mr. Tapping faced, from his superior, one hour later when the door had been opened, was distinctly unpleasant, and was not made the more agreeable from the fact that every rebuke resounded through the house, and carried joy and comfort to the listening boys.

The housemaster would hear no explanation; in fact, explanations were about the last thing he wanted. He desired to express his disgust, his indignation and his rage, and he did so magnificently.

"May I say one word, sir?" said Mr. Tapping in a lull.

"Quite unnecessary, Mr. Tapping," cut in the still angry master; "I don't wish any explanations. Such a thing as this has never happened in the history of this institution. That's all I wish to know. You forget that you are not left in charge of a young ladies' seminary."

"Very well, sir," said the mortified Mr. Tapping. "May I ask what you intend to do about this act of insubordination?"

" That is what I intend to ask *you*, sir," replied his superior. " Good-night."

The next day after luncheon, Mr. Tapping summoned the house to his study and addressed them as follows:

" Young gentlemen of the Dickinson House, I don't think you have any doubt as to why I have called you here. A very serious breach of discipline has taken place—one that cannot be overlooked. The sooner we meet the situation in the right spirit, gravely, with seriousness, the sooner will we meet each other in that spirit of harmony and friendly understanding that should exist between pupil and master. I am willing to make some allowance for the spirit of mischief, but none for an exhibition of untruthfulness. I warn you that I know, that I *know* who were the ringleaders in last night's outrage." Here he stopped and glanced in succession at each individual boy. Then suddenly turning, he said:

" Hicks, were you concerned in this? "

" Mr. Tapping," said Hickey, with the air of a martyr, " I refuse to answer."

" On what ground? "

" On the ground that I will not furnish any clue whatsoever."

" I shall deal with your case later."

" Very well, sir."

" Macnooder," continued Mr. Tapping, " what do you know about this? "

" I refuse to answer, sir."

At each demand, the same refusal.

Tapping, repulsed in his first attempt, hesitated and reflected. Above all things he did not wish to perpetuate last night's humiliation, and to continue the combat meant an accusation *en bloc* against the Dickinson House before the head master.

" Hicks, Macnooder and Reiter, wait here," he said suddenly; " the rest may go."

He walked up and down before the three a moment, and then said: " Reiter, you may go; you, too, Macnooder."

Hickey, thus deprived of all support, remained defiant.

" May I ask," he said indignantly, " why I am picked out? "

" Hicks," said Mr. Tapping sternly, without replying to the question, " I know pretty well who was the ringleader in this, and other things that have been going on in the past. I warn you, my boy, I shall keep my eye on you from this time forth.

That's all I want to say to you. Look out for yourself!"

Hickey could hardly restrain the tears. He went out with deadly wrath boiling in his heart. The idea of signalling him out from the whole house in that way! So then every hand was against him; he had no security; he was marked for suspicion, his downfall determined upon!

For one brief moment his spirit, the spirit of indomitable, battling boyhood, failed him, and he felt the grey impossibility of contending against tyrants. But only a moment, and then with a return of the old fighting spirit he suddenly conceived the idea of single-handed defying the whole organised hereditary and intrenched tyranny that sought to crush him, of matching his wits against the hydra despotism, perhaps, going down gloriously like Spartacus, for the cause, but leaving behind a name that should roll down the generations of future boys.

THE GREAT PANCAKE RECORD

LITTLE Smeed stood apart, in the obscure shelter of the station, waiting to take his place on the stage which would carry him to the great new boarding-school. He was frail and undersized, with a long, pointed nose and vacant eyes that stupidly assisted the wide mouth to make up a famished face. The scarred bag in his hand hung from one clasp, the premature trousers were at half-mast, while pink polka-dots blazed from the cuffs of his nervous sleeves.

By the wheels of the stage "Fire Crackers" Glendenning and "Jock" Hasbrouck, veterans of the Kennedy House, sporting the 'varsity initials on their sweaters and caps, were busily engaged in cross-examining the new boys who clambered timidly to their places on top. Presently, Fire Crackers, perceiving Smeed, hailed him.

"Hello, over there—what's your name?"

"Smeed, sir."

"Smeed what?"

"Johnnie Smeed."

The questioner looked him over with disfavour and said aggressively:

"You're not for the Kennedy?"

"No, sir."

"What house?"

"The Dickinson, sir."

"The Dickinson, eh? That's a good one," said Fire Crackers, with a laugh, and, turning to his companion, he added, "Say, Jock, won't Hickey and the old Turkey be wild when they get this one?"

Little Smeed, uncomprehending of the judgment

that had been passed, stowed his bag inside and clambered up to a place on the top. Jimmy, at the reins, gave a warning shout. The horses, stirred by the whip, churned obediently through the sideways of Trenton.

Lounging on the stage were half a dozen new-comers, six well-assorted types, from the well-groomed stripling of the city to the aggressive, big-limbed animal from the West, all profoundly under the sway of the two old boys who sat on the box with Jimmy and rattled on with quiet superiority. The coach left the outskirts of the city and rolled into the white highway that leads to Lawrenceville. The known world departed for Smeed. He gazed fearfully ahead, waiting the first glimpse of the new continent.

Suddenly Fire Crackers turned and, scanning the embarrassed group, singled out the strong Westerner with an approving glance.

"You're for the Kennedy?"

The boy, stirring uneasily, blurted out:

"Yes, sir."

"What's your name?"

"Tom Walsh."

"How old are you?"

" Eighteen."

" What do you weigh? "

" One hundred and seventy."

" Stripped? "

" What? Oh, no, sir—regular way."

" You've played a good deal of football? "

" Yes, sir."

Hasbrouck took up the questioning with a critical appreciation.

" What position? "

" Guard and tackle."

" You know Bill Stevens? "

" Yes, sir."

" He spoke about you; said you played on the Military Academy. You'll try for the 'varsity? "

" I guess so."

Hasbrouck turned to Fire Crackers in solemn conclave.

" He ought to stand up against Turkey if he knows anything about the game. If we get a good end we ought to give that Dickinson crowd the fight of their lives."

" There's a fellow came from Montclair they say is pretty good," Fire Crackers said, with solicitous gravity. " The line'll be all right if we can get some good halves. That's where the Dickinson has it on us."

Smeed listened in awe to the two statesmen studying out the chances of the Kennedy eleven for the house championship, realising suddenly that there were new and sacred purposes about his new life of which he had no conception. Then, absorbed by the fantasy of the trip and the strange unfolding world into which he was jogging, he forgot the lords of the Kennedy, forgot his fellows in ignorance, forgot that he didn't play football and was only a stripling, forgot everything but the fascination of the moment when the great school would rise out of the distance and fix itself indelibly in his memory.

"There's the water-tower," said Jimmy, extending the whip; "you'll see the school from the top of the hill."

Little Smeed craned forward with a sudden thumping of his heart. In the distance, a mile away, a cluster of brick and tile sprang out of the green, like a herd of red deer surprised in the forest. Groups of boys began to show on the roadside. Strange greetings were flung back and forth.

"Hello-oo, Fire Crackers!"

" How-de-do, Saphead! "

" Oh, there, Jock Hasbrouck! "

" Oh, you Morning Glory! "

" Oh, you Kennedys, we're going to lick you! "

" Yes you are, Dickinson! "

The coach passed down the shaded vault of the village street, turned into the campus, passed the ivy-clad house of the head master and rolled around a circle of well-trimmed lawn, past the long, low Upper House where the Fourth Form gazed at them in senior superiority; past the great brown masses of Memorial Hall and the pointed chapel, around to where the houses were ranged in red, extended bodies. Little Smeed felt an abject sinking of the heart at this sudden exposure to the thousand eyes fastened upon him from the wide esplanade of the Upper, from the steps of Memorial, from house, windows and stoops, from the shade of apple trees and the glistening road.

All at once the stage stopped and Jimmy cried: " Dickinson! "

At one end of the red-brick building, overrun with cool vines, a group of boys were lolling in flannels and light jerseys. A chorus went up.

" Hello, Fire Crackers! "

" Hello, Jock ! "

" Hello, you Hickey boy ! "

" Hello, Turkey ; see what we've brought you ! "

Smeed dropped to the ground amid a sudden hush.

" Fare," said Jimmy aggressively.

Smeed dug into his pocket and tendered the necessary coin. The coach squeaked away, while from the top Fire Crackers' exulting voice returned in insolent exultation :

" Hard luck, Dickinson ! Hard luck, you, old Hickey ! "

Little Smeed, his hat askew, his collar rolled up, his bag at his feet, stood in the road, alone in the world, miserable and thoroughly frightened. One path led to the silent, hostile group on the steps, another went in safety to the master's entrance. He picked up his bag hastily.

" Hello, you—over there ! "

Smeed understood it was a command. He turned submissively and approached with embarrassed steps. Face to face with these superior beings, tanned and muscular, stretched in Olympian attitudes, he realised all at once the hopelessness of his ever daring to associate with such demi-gods. Still he stood, shifting from foot to foot, eyeing the steps, waiting for

the solemn ordeal of examination and classification
to be over.

" Well, Hungry—what's your name? "

Smeed comprehended that the future was decided,
and that to the grave he would go down as " Hungry " Smeed. With a sigh of relief he answered:

" Smeed—John Smeed."

" Sir ! "

" Sir."

" How old? "

" Fifteen."

" Sir !! "

" Sir."

" What do you weigh? "

" One hundred and six—sir ! "

A grim silence succeeded this depressing information. Then some one in the back, as a mere matter
of form, asked:

" Never played football? "

" No, sir."

" Baseball? "

" No, sir."

" Anything on the track? "

" No, sir."

" Sing? "

" No, sir," said Smeed, humbly.

" Do anything at all? "

Little Smeed glanced at the eaves where the swallows were swaying and then down at the soft couch of green at his feet and answered faintly:

" No, sir—I'm afraid not."

Another silence came, then some one said, in a voice of deepest conviction:

" A dead loss! "

Smeed went sadly into the house.

At the door he lingered long enough to hear the chorus burst out:

" A fine football team we'll have! "

" It's a put-up job! "

" They don't want us to win the championship again—that's it! "

" I say, we ought to kick."

Then, after a little, the same deep voice:

" A dead loss! "

With each succeeding week Hungry Smeed comprehended more fully the enormity of his offence in doing nothing and weighing one hundred and six pounds. He saw the new boys arrive, pass through the fire of christening, give respectable weights and

go forth to the gridiron to be whipped into shape
by Turkey and the Butcher, who played on the school
eleven.   Smeed humbly and thankfully went down
each afternoon to the practice, carrying the sweaters and shin-guards, like the grateful little beast
of burden that he was.   He watched his juniors,
Spider and Red Dog, rolling in the mud or flung
gloriously under an avalanche of bodies; but then,
they weighed over one hundred and thirty, while
he was still at one hundred and six—a dead loss!
The fever of house loyalty invaded him; he even came
to look with resentment on the Faculty and to repeat secretly to himself that they never would have
unloaded him on the Dickinson if they hadn't been
willing to stoop to any methods to prevent the
House again securing the championship.

The fact that the Dickinson, in an extraordinary manner, finally won by the closest of margins,
consoled Smeed but a little while.   There were no
more sweaters to carry, or pails of barley water to
fetch, or guard to be mounted on the old rail-fence,
to make certain that the spies from the Davis and
Kennedy did not surprise the secret plays which
Hickey and Slugger Jones had craftily evolved.

With the long winter months he felt more keenly

his obscurity and the hopelessness of ever leaving a mark on the great desert of school-life that would bring honour to the Dickinson. He resented even the lack of the mild hazing the other boys received —he was too insignificant to be so honoured. He was only a " dead loss," good for nothing but to squeeze through his recitations, to sleep enormously, and to eat like a glutton with a hunger that could never be satisfied, little suspecting the future that lay in this famine of his stomach.

For it was written in the inscrutable fates that Hungry Smeed should leave a name that would go down imperishably to decades of schoolboys, when Dibbles' touchdown against Princeton and Kafer's home run should be only tinkling sounds. So it happened, and the agent of this divine destiny was Hickey.

It so happened that examinations being still in the threatening distance, Hickey's fertile brain was unoccupied with methods of facilitating his scholarly progress by homely inventions that allowed formulas and dates to be concealed in the palm and disappear obligingly up the sleeve on the approach of the Natural Enemy. Moreover, Hickey and Hickey's friends were in straitened circumstances, with all credit gone at the jigger-shop, and the appetite for jiggers in an acute stage of deprivation.

In this keenly sensitive, famished state of his imagination, Hickey suddenly became aware of a fact fraught with possibilities. Hungry Smeed had an appetite distinguished and remarkable even in that company of aching voids.

No sooner had this pregnant idea become his property than Hickey confided his hopes to Doc Macnooder, his chum and partner in plans that were dark and mysterious. Macnooder saw in a flash the glorious and lucrative possibilities. A very short series of tests sufficed to convince the twain that in little Smeed they had a phenomenon who needed only to be properly developed to pass into history.

Accordingly, on a certain muddy morning in March, Hickey and Doc Macnooder, with Smeed in tow, stole into the jigger-shop at an hour in defiance of regulations and fraught with delightful risks of detection.

Al, the watch-dog of the jigger, was tilted back, near a farther window, the parted tow hair falling doglike over his eyes, absorbed in the reading of Spenser's Faerie Queen, an abnormal taste which made him absolutely incomprehensible to the boyish mind. At the sound of the stolen entrance, Al put down the volume and started mechanically to rise. Then, recognising his visitors, he returned to his chair, saying wearily:

" Nothing doing, Hickey."

" Guess again," said Hickey, cheerily. " We're not asking you to hang us up this time, Al."

" You haven't got any money," said Al, the recorder of allowances; " not unless you stole it."

" Al, we don't come to take your hard-earned money, but to do you good," put in Macnooder impudently. " We're bringing you a little sporting proposition."

" Have you come to pay up that account of yours? " said Al. " If not, run along, you Macnooder; don't waste my time, with your wildcat schemes."

" Al, this is a sporting proposition," took up Hickey.

" Has *he* any money? " said Al, who suddenly remembered that Smeed was not yet under suspicion.

" See here, Al," said Macnooder, " we'll back Smeed to eat the jiggers against you—for the crowd! "

" Where's your money? "

" Here," said Hickey; " this goes up if we lose."

He produced a gold watch of Smeed's, and was about to tender it when he withdrew it with a sudden caution. "On the condition, if we win I get it back and you won't hold it up against my account."

"All right. Let's see it."

The watch was given to Al, who looked it over, grunted in approval, and then looked at little Smeed.

"Now, Al," said Macnooder softly, "give us a gambling chance; he's only a runt."

Al considered, and Al was wise. The proposition came often and he had never lost. A jigger is unlike any other ice cream; it is dipped from the creamy tin by a cone-shaped scoop called a jigger, which gives it an unusual and peculiar flavour. Since those days the original jigger has been contaminated and made ridiculous by offensive alliances with upstart syrups, meringues and macaroons with absurd titles; but then the boy went to the simple jigger as the sturdy Roman went to the cold waters of the Tiber. A double jigger fills a large soda-glass when ten cents has been laid on the counter, and two such glasses quench all desire in the normal appetite.

"If he can eat twelve double jiggers," Al said

slowly, " I'll set them up and the jiggers for youse. Otherwise, I'll hold the watch."

At this there was a protest from the backers of the champion, with the result that the limit was reduced to ten.

" Is it a go? " Al said, turning to Smeed, who had waited modestly in the background.

" Sure," he answered, with calm certainty.

" You've got nerve, you have," said Al, with a scornful smile, scooping up the first jiggers and shoving the glass to him. " Ten doubles is the record in these parts, young fellow! "

Then little Smeed, methodically, and without apparent pain, ate the ten doubles.

Conover's was not in the catalogue that anxious parents study, but then catalogues are like epitaphs in a cemetery. Next to the jigger-shop, Conover's was quite the most important institution in the school. In a little white Colonial cottage, Conover, veteran of the late war, and Mrs. Conover, still in active service, supplied pancakes and maple syrup on a cash basis, two dollars credit to second-year boys in good repute. Conover's, too, had its traditions. Twenty-six pancakes, large and thick, in one continuous sitting, was the record, five years old, standing to the credit of Guzzler Wilkins, which succeeding classes had attacked in vain. Wily Conover, to stimulate such profitable tests, had solemnly pledged himself to the delivery of free pancakes to all comers during that day on which any boy, at one continuous sitting, unaided, should succeed in swallowing the awful number of thirty-two. Conover was not considered a prodigal.

This deed of heroic accomplishment and public benefaction was the true goal of Hickey's planning. The test of the jigger-shop was but a preliminary trying out. With medical caution, Doc Macnooder refused to permit Smeed to go beyond the ten doubles, holding very wisely that the jigger record could wait for a further day. The amazed Al was sworn to secrecy.

It was Wednesday, and the following Saturday was decided upon for the supreme test at Conover's. Smeed at once was subjected to a graduated system of starvation. Thursday he was hungry, but Friday he was so ravenous that a watch was instituted on all his movements.

The next morning the Dickinson House, let into the secret, accompanied Smeed to Conover's. If there was even a possibility of free pancakes, the House intended to be satisfied before the deluge broke.

Great was the astonishment at Conover's at the arrival of the procession.

"Mr. Conover," said Hickey, in the quality of manager, "we're going after that pancake record."

"Mr. Wilkins' record?" said Conover, seeking vainly the champion in the crowd.

"No—after that record of *yours*," answered Hickey. "Thirty-two pancakes—we're here to get free pancakes to-day—that's what we're here for."

"So, boys, so," said Conover, smiling pleasantly; "and you want to begin now?"

"Right off the bat."

"Well, where is he?"

Little Smeed, famished to the point of tears, was thrust forward. Conover, who was expecting something on the lines of a buffalo, smiled confidently.

"So, boys, so," he said, leading the way with alacrity. "I guess we're ready, too."

"Thirty-two pancakes, Conover—and we get 'em free!"

"That's right," answered Conover, secure in his knowledge of boyish capacity. "If that little boy there can eat thirty-two I'll make them all day free to the school. That's what I said, and what I say goes—and that's what I say now."

Hickey and Doc Macnooder whispered the last instructions in Smeed's ear.

"Cut out the syrup."

"Loosen your belt."

"Eat slowly."

In a low room, with the white rafters impending over his head, beside a basement window flanked with geraniums, little Smeed sat down to battle for the honour of the Dickinson and the record of the school. Directly under his eyes, carved on the wooden table, a name challenged him, standing out of the numerous initials—Guzzler Wilkins.

"I'll keep count," said Hickey. "Macnooder and Turkey, watch the pancakes."

"Regulation size, Conover," cried that cautious Red Dog; "no doubling now. All fair and above-board."

"All right, Hickey, all right," said Conover, leering wickedly from the door; "if that little grasshopper can do it, you get the cakes."

"Now, Hungry," said Turkey, clapping Smeed on the shoulder. "Here is where you get your chance. Remember, Kid, old sport, it's for the Dickinson."

Smeed heard in ecstasy; it was just the way Turkey talked to the eleven on the eve of a match. He nodded his head with a grim little shake and smiled nervously at the thirty-odd Dickinsonians who formed around him a pit of expectant and hungry boyhood from the floor to the ceiling.

" All ready!" sang out Turkey, from the door-way.

" Six pancakes!"

" Six it is," replied Hickey, chalking up a monster 6 on the slate that swung from the rafters. The pancakes placed before the ravenous Smeed vanished like snow-flakes on a July lawn.

A cheer went up, mingled with cries of caution.

" Not so fast."

" Take your time."

" Don't let them be too hot."

" Not too hot, Hickey!"

Macnooder was instructed to watch carefully over the temperature as well as the dimensions.

" Ready again," came the cry.

" Ready—how many?"

" Six more."

" Six it is," said Hickey, adding a second figure to the score. " Six and six are twelve."

The second batch went the way of the first.

" Why, that boy is starving," said Conover, opening his eyes.

" Sure he is," said Hickey. " He's eating 'way back in last week—he hasn't had a thing for ten days."

" Six more," cried Macnooder.

" Six it is," answered Hickey. " Six and twelve is eighteen."

" Eat them one at a time, Hungry."

" No, let him alone."

" He knows best."

" Not too fast, Hungry, not too fast."

" Eighteen for Hungry, eighteen. Hurrah!"

" Thirty-two is a long ways to go," said Conover, gazing apprehensively at the little David who had come so impudently into his domain; " fourteen pancakes is an awful lot."

" Shut up, Conover."

" No trying to influence him there."

" Don't listen to him, Hungry."

" He's only trying to get you nervous."

" Fourteen more, Hungry—fourteen more."

" Ready again," sang out Macnooder.

"A stinging hand descended upon the crouching Piggy"

CALIFORNIA

" Oh, butter-fingers ! "

" Clumsy ! "

" Get your arms in to it ! "

" Now ! "

Warned by a chorus of instructions Moore strove a dozen times to retain the tantalising spinning oval, which constantly slipped his grasp with a smart reminder as it bounded away.

" My boy, your education has been neglected," said Jock in disgust. " At least try and learn how to fall on the ball. Watch."

Rolling the pigskin in front of him, he dove for it, pouncing on it as a beagle on a rabbit.

" Now, Piggy, let her go ! "

Moore, who loved his tailor-suit with the pride and affection which a father bestows only on the first-born, desperately essayed to secure the pigskin with the minimum of danger possible.

A shriek of derision burst forth.

" No, my dear Miss Moore, I did not ask you to lie down and pillow your head upon it," said Jock in disgust. " That is *not* what is called falling on the ball. Go at it like a demon; chew it up, mangle it ! Here, Morning Glory," he added, turning to a scrubby little urchin who was gambolling about,

" take this young lady and show her how it's done."

To Piggy's culminating mortification, the diminutive Morning Glory, with a contemptuous sneer, began to instruct him in the new art, with a rattling fire of insults which drew shrieks of laughter from the squad.

" Now then, old ice-wagon—get your nose in it."

" Don't spare the daisies, dearest."

" Jump, you Indian, jump!"

" Ah, watch me—like this."

The urchin hurled himself viciously on the ball, ploughing up the soft turf, and bounding gloriously to his feet, with scornful, mud-stained face, cried:

" Ah, what're you afraid of! Now then, old house-boat!"

Piggy's collar clung limply to his neck, half the buttons of his coat had gone, streaks of yellow and green decorated the suit a custom tailor had fashioned for fifty dollars cash, but still he was forced to go tumbling after the ball, down and up, up and down, head over heels, at the staccato shriek of the Morning Glory, like the one dog in the show who circles about the stage, tumbling somersaults.

" That's enough for to-day," came at last Jock's

welcome command. "We must begin easily. To-morrow we'll get into it. Practice over! Moore, jog around the circle six times and cut out pastry at supper."

During the dinner a great light dawned over Moore, as he sat silently investigating his new masters with sidelong, calculated glances. He went to his room and with one sweep eliminated the solid silver toilet set, removed the trees from his boots, packed away the pink embroidered bedroom slippers so neatly arranged under the bed and pruned solicitously among the gorgeous cravats. Then he went to the village and, under skilful prompting, bought a pair of corduroy trousers, a cap, a red-and-black jersey, the softest pair of football trousers in stock, a jersey padded at the elbows and shoulders, a sweater, a pair of heavy shoes, a nose protector, and a pair of shin-guards. Incased in every possible protection he reported next day for the dreadful ordeal of tackling and being tackled.

"So you've all got your togs," said Fire Crackers, surveying the squad of freshmen on the field. "Let's see how you made out."

With Keg Smith and Jock, he passed them over

in inspection, punching and poking the new suits with brief interjections, until Moore was reached. Before that swollen figure the three halted in mock amazement.

"Who's this?" said Keg, with a blank face.

"It's Moore, sir," said Piggy innocently.

"What's happened to you?" continued Fire Crackers with great seriousness.

Moore, perceiving he had blundered again, grew red with mortification, while Fire Crackers stripped the sweater from him and examined the jersey.

"Say, just see what Bill sold him!" he exclaimed. "Isn't it a shame how he'll impose on the green ones? Look at that bedticking! And those pads! Gee, I'll fix that!"

Before Moore could protest, Fire Crackers had ripped off the protections and flung them away.

"Now you'll feel easier," he said with a friendly smile. "Bill Appleby is an infernal old swindler: selling you shin-guards and a nose-protector! Huh! Throw 'em away."

"Thank you, sir," said Moore gratefully, "I'll make him take them back."

"That's right," said his inquisitor with a queer nod, "you're pretty green at this, aren't you?"

" I have **never** done much, sir."

" Well, let me give you a pointer; when you tackle, you want to grit your teeth and slam down hard, then you don't feel it at all."

" Thank you, sir."

" And when you're tackled," continued Fire Crackers with perfect seriousness, " just let yourself go limp; then you can't break any bones— see? "

" Yes, sir."

" You like the game, don't you? "

" Oh, very much."

Fire Crackers' advice did him scant good. On the whole it was probably the most painful afternoon he had ever known in his life. He had no instinct for tackling, that was certain. His arms slipped, his hands could not fasten to anything and he accomplished nothing more than to go sprawling, face downward.

" Funny you don't get on to that," said Jock, shaking his head. " I tell you what you do. Run down the line and take a few tackles; then you'll see how it's done."

Moore stood balancing, looking down to where Jock's one hundred and sixty-five pounds were gathering for a model tackle. Every natural instinct in him bade him turn tail and run.

"Come on now!" cried Jock, spitting on his hands. "Hard as you can."

Piggy went as a horse goes to a road-crusher, faltering and finally stopping dead. The next moment, Jock, cleaving the air in a perfect dive, caught him about the knees and threw him crashing to the ground. Piggy rose with difficulty.

"Do you get it now?" said Jock solicitously.

"I think I do," said Moore faintly.

"Well now, try one on me," said Jock, brightening. "Put your shoulder into it and squeeze it. Remember now."

Piggy remembered only the sensation of being tackled, and with the thought of that greater evil, improved astonishingly.

"That's the way to learn," said Jock approvingly. "Now, notice how I pull your legs from under you, and try to get that."

That evening after supper, Moore valiantly determined to take the bull by the horns. Seizing a favourable opportunity, he accosted his captain with the resolution of despair, and told him point blank that he would not be eligible for the team.

" Why not? " said Jock aggressively.

" I don't know anything about the game, sir," said Moore defiantly, " and I don't like it."

" Is that the only reason? "

" I don't want to play, sir—that ought to be enough."

" We're not *asking* you what you want to do."

" But, sir, I don't like it," said Moore, beginning to shrink under the cold, boring gaze of Hasbrouck.

" That has nothing to do with it, either."

" Nothing——"

" Certainly not. We don't want you; in fact, we're crying because we've got to take you. You're a flub-dub and a quitter. But there's no one else, and so, Piggy, mark you—we're going to make a demon out of you, a regular demon. Mark my words! "

All of which was accomplished easily and naturally within a short two weeks by the discipline and tradition which has put courage into the hearts of generations of natural cowards.

The crisis came in the first game of the series; when for the first time, Piggy beheld the terrifying spectacle of an end run started in his direction. At the sight of the solid front of bone and muscle ready to sweep him off his feet and send him tumbling head over heels, he shut his eyes and funked deliberately and ingloriously.

The next moment Jock had him by the small of the neck; Jock's hand jerked him to his feet and Jock's voice cried:

"You cowardly little pup! You do that again and I'll tear the hide off you!"

Piggy, chilled to the bone, went to his position. The opposing team, with a shout of exultation, sent the same play crashing in his direction. Piggy, desperate with fear, tore through the advancing mass, found the runner and hurled him to the ground. Jock smiled contentedly. Moore was a coward, he knew, but from that time forth, no passing menace before him could compare with the abiding terror that waited behind.

Had Moore been possessed of even moderate courage the task would have been difficult, for then it would have resolved itself into a mere question of natural ability. But being an arrant and utter coward, his very cowardice drove him into feats of desperate recklessness. For always, in lull or storm, in the confusion of the mêlée or the open scramble down the field to cover a punt, Moore felt the ominous presence of Hasbrouck just at his shoulder and heard the sharp and threatening cry:

" Get that man, you, Piggy! "

So blindly and rebelliously he served the tyrant, and unwilling and revolting learned to despise fear, little suspecting how many reckless spirits of other teams had been formed under the same rude discipline.

The earlier contests developed the strength of the two long-time rivals, the Kennedy and the Dickinson, between whom at last lay the question of supremacy. The last week approached with excitement at fierce heat. Every day a fresh rumour was served up; Hickey, the wily Dickinson quarter, had a weak ankle; Turkey, the captain, was behind in his studies; a Princeton 'varsity man was over, coaching the enemy; the signals were discovered and a dozen trick plays were being held in reserve, each good for a touchdown.

Each night on the Kennedy steps, the council of war convened and plans were discussed in utter gravity for temporarily crippling and eliminating from the contest Turkey, Slugger-Jones, Hickey and the Butcher. For, of course, it was conceded that Jock, Tom Walsh and Fire Crackers would probably be maimed for life by the brutal and unscrupulous enemy.

Piggy, whose critical sense of humour had been under early disadvantages, took this as exact truth and beheld the horrible day arrive with an absolute conviction that it would be his last. He did not sleep during the night; he could eat nothing during the day; his fingers trembled and snarled up the lacings as he forced himself into his football clothes. Then he stood a long moment, viewing his white face in the mirror—the last look, perhaps—and went weakly to join the squad below. He heard nothing of the magnificent address of Jock to his followers; one idea only was in his head: to sell his life as dearly as possible.

While the captains conferred and tossed for position, the two teams, face to face at last, paced up and down, eyeing each other with contempt, breathing forth furious threats.

The Egghead assured Fatty Harris that the first scrimmage would be his last. Fatty Harris returned the compliment and suggested that the Egghead leave a memorandum for the hearse. The Coffee Cooler looked Buffalo Brown over and sneered;

Keg Smith did as much to the Butcher and laughed. The diminutive Spider at right end, approached his dear friend Legs Brockett, his opponent, and muttered through his teeth:

"I'm going to slug you!"

While these friendly salutations were taking place, Flea Obie and Wash Simmons, the Dickinson halves, approached Piggy, who, sick at heart, was stamping his feet and churning his arms to convey to Red Dog, opposite, the impression that he was thirsting for his blood.

Wash gave Piggy one withering glance and said loudly to the Red Dog:

"This fellow's a quitter. He's got yellow in his eyes. Smash him good and hard, Red Dog. Don't waste any time about it, either."

"He's got a chicken liver," said Red Dog, who looked a reed beside the sturdy Piggy. "He shuts his eyes when he tackles! I'll fix him. Huh!"

"Ah, go on now; go on, go on," said Piggy, with a desperate attempt at lightheartedness.

Flea Obie, lovely no longer in mud-stained jacket and pirate band around his forehead, strode up to Piggy and added:

"Old Sport, let me give you a word of advice. When we strike your end, the best thing you can do is to lie down *quick and soft. Savez?* "

Luckily for Piggy, whose imagination was panic-driven by this perfectly innocuous braggadocio, the torrent of conversation was checked by a cry of exultation.

The Kennedy had won the toss and chose the kick-off. Bat Finney, umpire from the Fourth Form, called the two teams together and said solemnly:

"Now I want it understood by you fellows this is going to be a gentleman's game. No roughing it, no slugging, nothing bru-tal. Take your sides."

Immediately the air resounded with war cries:

"Get in there, Dickinson."

"Chew 'em up, Kennedy."

"Hit 'em hard, Buffalo."

"Sock 'em, Turkey."

"Knock 'em out, boys!"

Piggy, at left end with his eye on the ball, waited hopelessly for Jock to send the oval spinning into Dickinson territory. He was shivering, in a dead funk. The whistle blew, the run was on. Piggy went perfunctorily, helplessly down the field to where the dreaded Hickey, ball under arm, was dodging toward him. Suddenly the vigorous form of Wash Simmons hove into view, headed directly for him. He wavered and the next moment was knocked off his feet, while Hickey, the way thus cleared for him, went bounding back for a run of forty yards.

Meanwhile Piggy was in the hands of Jock, who administered to him before the eyes of every spectator, a humiliating and well-placed kick.

"You funked, I saw you funk, you miserable shivery little coward!" he cried, shaking his fist in his face. "You jump in there now and cripple a few of those fellows or I'll massacre you!"

He added a few words which shall remain sacred between them and shoved him into place. The old fear awoke triumphant in Piggy. He rushed in like a demon, whirling over the field, upsetting play after play, making tackles that brought Flea Obie and Wash Simmons to their feet rubbing their sides. Nothing could stop him, for at last he was panic-stricken, utterly and horribly afraid.

The two teams, evenly matched, fought each other to a standstill. The first half closed without any perceptible advantage. The second half continued the deadlock, the precious minutes slipping away. Such a struggle had never been known in a House contest. Several eyes were closed, several bandages had appeared. The frenzy of battle had taken possession of the descendants of Goth and Viking. Challenges to future encounters were flung recklessly and recklessly accepted. After each mêlée little clusters of battling boyhood were disentangled with difficulty, while Bat Finney, the umpire, joyfully proclaimed:

"No roughing it, fellows—remember, this is a *gentleman's* game."

The dusk began to cloud the field and the players, one of those tragic, melancholy mists that come only at the close of a desperate second half. Two minutes only to play and the ball in the Kennedy's possession, exactly at midfield, without a score.

"6-5-8-15-2-3!" shrieked Fire Crackers, grimy and unrecognisable.

The team, converging swiftly for a revolving mass play on tackle, strove wearily to make headway against the reeling Dickinsons, who, too fagged to upset the play, could only hold, surging and twisting. Piggy, scrambling and pushing, head down in the mêlée, whirled and spun with the revolving mass. Then his feet tripped and he went underneath, shielding his head from the vortex of legs that swirled

above him. Suddenly, lying free, a scant five yards
in front of him, he perceived, to his horror, the
precious ball! With a lurch, he freed himself from
the mass, scrambled to his feet, picked up the ball
and set out, break-a-neck, for the far-away goal.
Five yards behind was Hickey, the fleet quarter,
bounding after him.

In a twinkling the whole scene had changed into
the extraordinary spectacle of a stern chase, two
figures well in front, striving for the mastery of the
fates, and behind the futile, scrambling, exulting, or
desperate mass of players, sweeping helplessly on
the tracks of destiny.

Forty yards to the interminable goal! Piggy remembered with dread the stories of Hickey's fleetness.
He glanced back. His pursuer had not gained an
inch. On the contrary, his freckled face was dis-
torted, his arms were churning, his teeth were horribly displayed, biting at the stinging air, with the
agony of the effort to increase his speed. So he
was beating out Hickey, the famous Hickey! Then
the touchdown was a fact! Above the uproar he
heard a strident shriek:

"Piggy, oh, you damned Piggy!"

The terror of that familiar voice gave a new impetus to his chubby legs. Some one else must be gaining on him. Thirty yards still to go!

He ran and ran, hugging the ball in his arms, his head thrown back, gasping for breath. Twenty yards — fifteen yards! Suddenly swift, glorious visions rose before him, scenes of jubilation and exultation, of cheering comrades, celebrations that would wipe out the long record of humiliation. Hickey was closer now, but Piggy did not dare to turn his head; five yards more and the game would be over and the kingdom of the Kennedy in his grasp. He sped over the last white chalk line and dropped triumphant behind the goal posts. The next moment, Hickey, wily Hickey, screaming with laughter, flung himself on him.

Piggy gazed about wildly with a sudden horrible suspicion. He had run over his own goal line and scored a safety for the Dickinson.

Then Hasbrouck arrived.

THE FUTURE PRESIDENT

"Snorky" Green, at the fourth desk of the middle aisle, gazed dreamily at the forgotten pages of the divine Virgil. The wide windows let in the warm breath of June meadows and the tiny sounds of contented insects roaming in unhuman liberty. Outside were soft banks to loll upon, from which to watch the baseball candidates gambolling over the neat diamond, tennis courts calling to be played upon, and the friendly "jigger" ready to soothe the parched highway to the aching void. And for an hour the tugging souls of forty-two imprisoned little pagans would have to construe, and parse, and decline, se-

cretly cursing the fossils who rediscovered those unnecessary Latin documents.

Eight rows of desks, nine deep, were swept by the
Argus eye of the master from his raised pulpit.
Around the room, immense vacant blackboards shut
them in—dark, hopeless walls over which no convict
might clamber, on which a thousand boys had blundered and guessed and writ in water.

Lucius Cassius Hopkins, "The Roman," man of
heroic and consular mould, flunker of boys, and de-
viser of systems against which even the ingenuity
of a Hickey hurled itself in vain, sat on the rostrum,
pitilessly mowing down the unresisting ranks.

Snorky's tousled hair was more rumpled than ever,
a smudge was on one cheek, where his grimy, ball-
stained hand had unknowingly left its mark. He
was dirty, bored, and unprepared. The dickey at
his throat, formed by the junction of a collar and
two joined cuffs, saved the proprieties and allowed
the body to keep cool. But the spirit of dreams was
upon Snorky, and the hard, rectangular room began
to recede.

He heard indistinctly the low, mocking rumble of
the Roman as his scythe passed down the rows.

" Anything from the Simpson twins to-day? No,

no? Anything from the Davis House combination? Too bad! too bad! Nothing from the illuminating Hicks? Yes? No? Too bad! too bad!"

Snorky did not hear him; his eyes were on the firm torsos of Flash Condit and Charley De Soto before him—Condit, wonder of the football field, hero of the touchdown against the Princeton 'varsity, and De Soto the phenomenal shortstop, both Olympian spirits doomed to endure the barbed shafts of Lucius Cassius Hopkins.

He, too,—Snorky,—would go down in the annals of school history. He remembered the beginning of an out-curve he had developed that morning in the lot back of the Woodhull—a genuine out-curve, Ginger Pop Rooker to the contrary, notwithstanding. With a little practice he would master the perplexing in-curve and the drop. And the Woodhull needed a pitcher badly. McCarthy had no courage; the Dickinson would batter him all over the field in the afternoon's game, and then good-bye to the championship. In his mind he began the game, trotting hopelessly out into left field. He saw Hickey, first up for the Dickinson, get a base on balls—four wide ones in succession. Slugger Jones, four balls—heavens, to be beaten like that! Turkey Reiter, third man up, hit a two-bagger; two runs. Doc Macnooder knocked the first ball pitched for a clean single; a two-bagger for the Egghead! Again four balls for Butcher Stevens! The Red Dog, of all people in the world, to hit safely! And still they allowed the slaughter to go on! The Dickinson House was shrieking with joy, dancing war-dances, back of third, and singing derisive songs of triumph. Flea Obie went to first on another base on balls, filling the bases. And five runs over the plate! Hickey and Turkey on the line began to dance a cake-walk. From the uproarious Dickinsonians rose the humiliating wail:

> "We're on to his curves, we're on to his curves;
> Long-legged McCarthy has lost his nerves."

McCarthy *had* lost his nerves. Five runs, the bases full, and "Wash" Simmons, the Dickinson pitcher, to the bat. The infield, badly rattled, played in to catch the runner at home in approved professional style. Snorky stole in closer and closer until he was almost back of shortstop. Simmons he knew couldn't send it out of the diamond. But Wash knocked what looked to be a clean single, clear over the heads of the near infield. That was what he had been waiting for; on the full run he made a desperate dive, caught the ball one-handed, close to the ground, turned a somersault, scrambled to second base, and shot the ball to first before the runner could even check himself!

Nothing like it had ever been seen in Lawrenceville. Even the Dickinsons generously applauded him as he came up happy and flushed.

"Snorky, that's the greatest play I ever saw pulled off. I wish I had made it myself."

He looked up. The speaker was the dashing De Soto. That from Charley, the greatest ball-player who ever came to Lawrenceville! Snorky's throat swelled with emotion. At last they knew his worth.

One run for the Woodhull. Again the Dickinsons to the bat, and again the rout; one single, a base on balls, two bases on balls—oh, if he only would get his chance! One ball, two balls, three balls. Suddenly McCarthy stopped and clutched his arm with an exclamation of pain. The team gathered about him. Snorky sniffed in disdain; he knew that trick, pretending it was all on account of his arm! What a quitter McCarthy was, after all! Still, what was to be done? The team gathered in grave discussion. No one else had ever pitched.

" Give me a chance," he said suddenly to " Rock " Bemis, the captain.

" You!" said Rock, with a laugh; " you, Snorky!"

" Look at me! I can do it," he answered, and met the other's glare with steady look as heroes do. Something of the fire in that look convinced Bemis.

" Why not? " he said. " The game's gone, anyhow. Go into the box, Snorky, and put them over if you can."

The teams lined up. With clenched teeth and a cold streak down his spine he strode into the box. An insulting yelp went up from the enemy.

Three balls, no strikes, and the bases full! Turkey at the plate stepped back scornfully to wait for the fourth ball.

" Strike one!"

Turkey advanced to the utmost limit of the batter's box, turned his back deliberately on Snorky, and called out:

" You hit me, and I'll break your neck!"

" Strike two!"

Turkey turned in surprise, looked at him, and deliberated.

" He can't put it over," yelled the gallery. " Yi, yi, yi!"

Then Turkey seated himself Indian fashion, his back still to Snorky, and gazed up into the face of " Tug " Moffat, the catcher. A furious wrangle ensued, the Woodhull claiming that his position was illegal, the Dickinson insisting that nothing in the rules prohibited it. " Stonewall " Jackson, the umpire, a weak-minded fellow from the Rouse House, allowed the play.

" Strike three!"

Turkey, crestfallen and muttering, arose and dusted himself amid the jeers of the onlookers. Doc Macnooder smote high and low, and then forgot to smite—three strikes and out. The Egghead, despite the entreaties of the Dickinson to bring in his housemates, could only foul out. The Woodhulls went wild with delight. He heard Tug, the catcher, whispering excitedly to De Soto.

" Charley, just watch him! He's got everything —everything!"

Then the Woodhull tied the score on two bases on balls, and his own two-bagger.

When he walked lightly into the box for the third inning, Stonewall Jackson had been replaced by De

Soto with the imperious remark: "Here, get out! I want to watch this."

He gave the great Charley a modest nod.

"When did you ever pitch?" said De Soto, critically.

"Oh, now and then," he answered.

"Well, Snorky, let yourself out."

"Tug can't hold me," he said impudently. "That's the trouble, Charley."

"Try him."

Tug signalled for an in-shoot. He wound himself up and let fly. Butcher Stevens flung himself from the plate, Moffat threw up his mit in sudden fear. The ball caromed off and went frolicking past the back-stop.

"Strike one!"

Tug, puzzled and apprehensive, came up for a consultation.

"Gee! Snorky, give me warning! What do you think I am—a Statue of Liberty?"

"Charley wants me to let myself out. I'll slow down on the third strike," he said loftily. "Let the others go if you want."

Tug, like a Roman gladiator, with undying resolve, squatted back of the plate and signalled for an out. No use; no mit of his could ever stop the frightful velocity of that shoot.

" Stri-ike two! "

" Now ease up a bit," cautioned De Soto.

He sent a floating out-drop that seemed headed for Butcher Stevens's head, and finally settled gently over the plat at the waist-line.

" Striker out! "

Moffat no longer tried to hold him, admitting himself outclassed by the blinding speed of ins and outs, jump balls, and cross fire that Snorky hurled unerringly across the plate. The Red Dog and Flea Obie, plainly unnerved, died like babes in their tracks. Five strike-outs in two innings!

Then De Soto spoke.

" Here, Snorky, you get out of this! "

A cry of protest came from the Woodhull.

" Yell all you like," said De Soto; " Snorky is going with me where he belongs."

And, to the amazement of the two houses, he drew his arm under Snorky's and marched him right over to the 'varsity diamond.

How the school buzzed and chattered about the phenomenal rise of the new pitcher! He saw himself pitching wonderful curves to burly " Cap " Kiefer, the veteran back-stop, built like a mastodon, who had all he could do to hold those frightful balls. He saw the crowds of boys, six deep, who stood reverentially between times to watch the amazing curves. He heard pleasurably the chorus of " Ahs! " and " Ohs! " and " Gees! " which followed each delivery. Then suddenly he was in the box on the great, clean diamond, with the eyes of hundreds of boys fastened prayerfully on him, and the orange-and-black stripes of a Princeton 'varsity man facing him at the plate. To beat the Princeton 'varsity—what a goal!

He saw each striped champion come up gracefully and retire crestfallen to the bench, even as the Dickinson batters had done. Inning after inning passed without a score; not a Princeton man reached first. Then in the seventh an accident happened. The first Princeton man up deliberately stepped into the ball, and the umpire allowed him to take his base. It was outrageous, but worse was to follow. On the attempt to steal second, Cap lined a beautiful ball to the base, but no one covered it—a mistake in signals! And the runner kept on to third! Snorky settled down and struck out the next two batters. The Lawrenceville bleachers rose *en masse* and shrieked his praises. Then suddenly Kiefer, to catch the runner off third, snapped the ball to Waladoo a trifle, just a trifle, wild; but the damage was done. 1 to 0 in favor of Princeton. Even the great Princeton captain, Barrett, said to him:

"Hard luck, Green! Blamed hard luck!"

But Snorky wasn't beaten yet. The eighth and ninth innings passed without another Princeton man reaching first. Nine innings without a hit—wonderful!—and yet to be beaten by a fluke. One out for Lawrenceville; two out. The third man up, Cap Kiefer himself, reached first on an error. "Green to the bat," sung out the scorer.

Snorky looked around, picked up his bat, and calmly strode to the plate. He had no fear; he knew what was going to happen. One ball, one strike, two strikes. He let the drop pass. What he wanted was a swift in-shoot. Two balls—too high. Three balls—wide of the plate. He was not to be tempted by any such. Two strikes and three balls; now he must get what he wanted. He cast one glance at the bleachers, alive with the frantic red-and-black flags; he heard his comrades calling, beseeching, imploring. Then his eye settled on the far green stretch between right and centre field and the brown masses of Memorial, where no ball before had ever reached. A home run would drive in Kiefer and win the game! The chance had come. The Princeton pitcher slowly began to wind up for the delivery. Snorky settled into the box, caught his bat with the grip of desperation, gathered together all his sinews, and——

"Green!" called the sharp, jeering voice of Lucius Cassius Hopkins.

Snorky sprang to his feet in fright, clutching at his book. The great home run died in the air.

"Translate."

Snorky gazed helplessly at the page, seeking the place. He heard the muffled voice of Hickey behind him whisper:

"The advance, the advance, you chump!"

But to find the place under the hawk eyes of the Roman was an impossibility. He stared at the page in a well-simulated attempt, shook his head, and sat down.

"A very creditable attempt, Green," said the master, now with a gentle voice. "De Soto?—Nothing from De Soto? Dear, dear! We'll have to try

Macnooder then. What? Studied the wrong lesson? How sad! Mistakes will happen. Don't want to try that, either? No feeling of confidence to-day; no feeling of confidence." He began to call them by rows. " Dark, Davis, Denton, Dibble— nothing in the D's. Farr, Francis, Frey, Frick— nothing from the F's; nothing from the D. F's. Very strange! very strange! Little spring fever— yes? Too bad! too bad! Lesson too long? Yes? Too long to get any of it? Dear! dear! Every one studied the review, I see. Excellent moral idea, conscientious; wouldn't go on until you have mastered yesterday's lesson. Well, well, so we'll have a beautiful recitation in the review."

How absurd it was to be flunking under the Roman! Next year he would show them. He would rise early in the morning and study hours before breakfast; he would master everything, absorb everything—declensions and conjugations, Greek, Roman, and mediæval civilisation; he would frolic in equations and toy with logarithms; his translation would be the wonder of the faculty. He would crush Red Dog and Crazy Opdyke; he would be valedictorian of his class. They would speak of him as a phenomenon, as a prodigy, like Pascal—was it Pascal? What a tribute the head master would pay him at commencement! There on the stage before all the people, the fathers and mothers and sisters, before the Red Dog, and Ginger Pop Rooker, and Hickey, and all the rest, sitting open-mouthed while he, Snorky Green, the crack pitcher and valedictorian of his class, a scholar such as Lawrenceville had never known—

"Green, Gay, and Hammond, go to the board. Take your books."

Snorky went hastily and clumsily, waiting as a gambler waits for his chance.

"Gay, decline his, hæc, hoc; Green, write out the gerundive forms of all the verbs in the first paragraph top of page 163."

Snorky gazed helplessly at the chronicles of Æneas, and then blankly at the inexorable blackboard, where so many gerundives had not been inscribed.

He drew his name in lagging letters exactly midway, at the top, with a symmetrical space above.

R. B. GREEN

Then he searched anxiously for the gerundives that lurked somewhere in the first paragraph, top of page

163. Then returning to the board he rubbed out the name with little reluctant dabs and wrote

ROGER B. GREEN

Abandoning the chase for gerundives, he stood off a few feet and surveyed his labours on the blackboard, frowned, erased it and wrote dashingly,

ROGER BALLINGTON GREEN

Satisfied, he drew a strong line under it, added two short crosses and a dot or two, and returned to his seat.

Once more in the abode of dreams he was transported to college, president of his class, the idol of his mates, the marvel of the faculty. He hesitated on the border-line of a great football victory, where, single-handed, bruised, and suffering, he would win the game for his college;—and then found higher levels. War had been declared swiftly and treacherously by the German Empire. The whole country was rising to the President's call to arms. A great meeting of the University was held, and he spoke with a sudden revelation of a power for oratory he had never before suspected.

That very afternoon a company was formed under his leadership. Twenty-four hours later they marched to the station, and, amid a whirlwind of cheers and godspeeds, embarked for the front. During the night, while others slept, he pored over books of tactics; he studied the campaigns of Cæsar, Napoleon, Grant, and Moltke. In the first disastrous year of the war, when the American army was beaten back at every point and an invading force of Germans was penetrating from the coast in three sections, he rose to the command of his regiment, with the reputation of being the finest disciplinarian in the army. Their corps was always at the front, checking the resistless advance of the enemy, saving their comrades time after time at frightful loss. Then came that dreadful day when it seemed as though the Army of the South was doomed to be surrounded and crushed by the sudden tightening of the enemy's net before the Army of the Centre could effect a junction. In the gloomy council he spoke out. One way of escape there was, but it meant the sacrifice of five thousand men. Clearly and quickly he traced his plan, while general, brigadier-general, and general-in-chief stared in amazement at the new genius that flashed before their minds.

"That is the plan," he said calmly, with the authority of a master mind; "it means the safety of a hundred thousand, and if a junction can be made with the Army of the Centre, the Germans can be stopped and driven back at so-and-so. But this means the death of five thousand men. There is only one man who has the right to die so—the man who proposes it. Give me five regiments, and I will hold the enemy for thirty-six hours."

He threw his regiments boldly into the enemy's line of march, and by a sudden rush carried the spur that dominated the valley. The German army, surprised and threatened in its most vulnerable spot, forced to abandon the pursuit, turned to crush the handful of heroes.

All day long the desperate battalions flung themselves in vain against the little band. All day long he walked with drawn sword up and down the thinning ranks, stiffening their courage. Red Dog and Ginger Pop called to him, imploring him not to expose himself—Red Dog and Ginger Pop, whose idol he now was; yes, and Hickey's and Condit's, too. But carelessly, defiantly, he stood in full view, his clothes pierced, his head bared. Then came the night—the long, fatiguing night, without an instant's cessation. The carnage was frightful. Half of the force gone, and twelve hours more to hold out! That was his promise.   And the sickening dawn, with the shrouded clouds and the expectant vultures, came stealing out of the East.   Until night came again they must cling to the spur-top and manage to live in that hurricane of lead.   He went down the line, calling each man by name, rousing them, like a prophet inspired.   The fury of sacrifice seized them. They fought on, parched and bleeding, while the sun rose above them and slowly fell.   A thousand lives; half that, and half that again.   Five o'clock, and still two hours to go.   He looked about him.   Only a few hundred remained to meet the next charge. Red Dog and Ginger Pop were cold in death, Hickey was dying.   Of all his school friends, only Flash Condit remained, staggering at his side.   And then the great masses of the enemy swept over them like an avalanche, and he fell, unconscious but happy, with the vision of martyrdom shining above him.

Red Dog, on his way back to his seat, knocked against him, saying angrily:

"All day long he walked with drawn sword"

" Oh, you clumsy! "

Red Dog, of all the world! Red Dog, whom he had just cheered into a hero's death. Snorky, thus brought to earth, decided to resuscitate himself and read the papers, with their big page-broad scareheads of the fight on the spur. This accomplished, he decided to end the war. The President, driven by public clamour, put him in command of the Army of the South. In three weeks, by a series of rapid Napoleonic marches, he flung the enemy into morasses and wilderness, cut their line of communication, and starved them into surrender; then flinging his army north, he effected a junction with the Army of the Centre, sending a laconic message to the President: " I am here. Give me command, and I will feed the sea with the remnants of Germany's glory."

Official Washington, intriguing and jealous, cried out for a court-martial; but the voice of the people, echoing from coast to coast, gave him his wish. In one month he swept the middle coast bare of resistance, fought three enormous battles, and annihilated the armies of the invaders, ending the war. What a triumph was his! That wonderful entry into Washington, with the frenzied roars of multitudes that greeted him, as he rode simply and modestly, but greatly, down the Avenue at the head of his old regiment, in their worn and ragged uniforms, with the flag shot to shreds proudly carried by the resuscitated Hickey and Flash Condit, seeing in the crowd the tear-stained faces of the Roman and the head master and all his old comrades, amid the waving handkerchiefs of frantic thousands.

At this point Snorky's emotion overmastered him. A lump was in his throat. He controlled himself with difficulty and dignity. He went over the quiet, stately years until a grateful nation carried him in triumph into the Presidential chair, nominated by acclamation and without opposition! He saw the wonderful years of his ascendency, the wrongs righted, peace and concord returning to all classes, the development of science, the uniting into one system of all the warring branches of education, the amalgamation of Canada and Mexico into the United States, the development of an immense merchant fleet, the consolidation of all laws into one national code, the establishment of free concerts and theatres for the people. Then suddenly there fell a terrible blow, the hand of a maniac struck him down as he passed through the multitudes who loved him. He was carried unconscious to the nearest house. The greatest physicians flocked to him, striving in vain to fight off the inevitable end. He saw the street filled with tan-bark and the faces of the grief-stricken multitude, with Hickey and Red Dog and Ginger Pop sobbing on the steps and refusing to leave all that fateful night, while bulletins of the final struggle were constantly sent to every part of the globe. And then he died. He heard the muffled peal of bells, and the sobs that went up from every home in the land; he saw the houses being decked with crape, and the people, with aching hearts, trooping into the churches: for he, the President, the beloved, the great military genius, the wisest of human rulers, was dead—dead.

Suddenly a titter, a horrible, mocking laugh, broke through the stately dignity of the national grief. Snorky, with tears trembling in his eyes, suddenly brought back to reality, looked up to see Lucius Cassius Hopkins standing over him with mocking smile. From their desks Red Dog and Hickey were making faces at him, roaring at his discomfiture.

"So Green is dreaming again! Dear, dear! Dreaming again!" said the deliberate voice. "Dreaming of chocolate éclairs and the jigger-shop, eh, Green?"

FURTHER PERSECUTION OF HICKEY

EVER since the disillusionising encounter with Tabby, Hickey, like the obscure Bonaparte before the trenches of Toulon, walked moodily alone, absorbed in his own resolves, evolving his immense scheme of a colossal rebellion. Macnooder, alone, received the full confidence of the war *à outrance* with the faculty which he gradually evolved.

Macnooder was the man of peace, the Mazarin and the Machiavelli of the Dickinson. He risked nothing in action, but to his cunning mind with its legal sense of dangers to be met and avoided, were brought all the problems of conspiracies against the discipline of the school. Macnooder pronounced the scheme of a revolt heroic, all the more so that he saw an opportunity of essaying his strategy on large lines.

"We must begin on a small scale, Hickey," he said wisely, "and keep working up to something really big."

"I thought we might organise a secret society," said Hickey, ruminating, "something masonic, all sworn to silence and secrecy and all that sort of thing."

"No," said Doc, "just as few as possible and no real confidants, Hickey; we'll take assistants as we need them."

"What would you begin with?"

"We must strike a blow at Tabby," said Macnooder. "We must show him that we don't propose to stand for any of his underhanded methods."

"He needs a lesson," Hickey asserted savagely.

"How about the skeleton?"

"Humph!" said Hickey, considering; "perhaps, but that's rather old."

" Not up the flag-pole—something new."

" What is it, Doc? "

Hickey looked at Macnooder with expectant admiration.

" I noticed something yesterday in Memorial, during chapel, that gave me an idea," said Macnooder profoundly. " There is a great big ventilator in the ceiling; now there must be some way of getting to that and letting a rope down." Macnooder stopped and looked at Hickey. Hickey returned a look full of admiration, then by a mutual movement they clasped hands in ecstatic, sudden delight.

That night they reconnoitred with the aid of a dark-lantern, borrowed from Legs Brownell of the Griswold, and the pass-keys, of which Hickey was the hereditary possessor.

They found to their delight that there was in fact a small opening through which one boy could wriggle with difficulty.

The attempt was fixed for the following night, and as a third boy was indispensable it was decided that etiquette demanded that the owner of the lantern should have the first call.

At two o'clock that night Hickey and Macnooder

stole down the creaking stairs, and out Sawtelle's window (the highway to the outer world). The night was misty, with a pleasant, ghostly chill that heightened measurably the delight of the adventure. In the shadow of the Griswold a third shivering form cautiously developed into the possessor of the dark-lantern.

After a whispered consultation, they proceeded to Foundation House, where they secured the necessary rope from the clothes-line, it being deemed eminently fitting to secure the coöperation of the best society.

Memorial Hall entered, they soon found themselves, by the aid of the smelly lantern, in front of the closet that held the skeleton which twice a week served as demonstration to the class in anatomy, and twice a year was dragged forth to decorate the flag-pole or some such exalted and inaccessible station. In a short time the door yielded to the prying of the hatchet Macnooder had thoughtfully brought along, and the white, chalky outlines of the melancholy skeleton appeared.

The three stood gazing, awed. It was black and still, and the hour of the night when dogs howl and bats go hunting.

"Who's going to take him?" said Legs in a whisper.

"Take it yourself," said Macnooder, unhooking the wriggling form. "Hickey's got to crawl through the air hole, and I've got to work the lantern. You're not superstitious, are you?"

"Sure, I'm not," retorted Legs, who received the skeleton in his arms with a shiver that raised the goose-flesh from his crown to his heels.

"Come on," said Hickey in a whisper; "softly now."

"What's that?" exclaimed Legs, drawing in his breath.

"That's nothing," said Macnooder loftily; "all buildings creak at night."

"I swear I heard a step. There again. Listen."

"Legs is right," said Hickey in a whisper. "It's outside."

"Rats! it's nothing but Jimmy," said Macnooder with enforced calm. "Keep quiet until he passes on."

They stood breathless until the sounds of the watchman on his nightly rounds died away. Then they started on tiptoes up the first flight for the chapel, Macnooder leading with the lantern, Legs next with the skeleton gingerly carried in his arms, Hickey bringing up the rear with the coil of rope.

"Here we are," said Macnooder at length. "Legs, you wait here,—see, that's where we're going to hoist him." He flashed the bull's-eye upward to the perforated circle directly above the rostrum, and added: "I'll get Hickey started and then I'll be right back."

"Are you going to take the lantern?" said Legs, whose courage began to fail him.

"Sure," said Hickey, indignantly. "Legs, you're getting scared."

"No, I'm not," protested Legs, faintly, "but I don't like to be left all alone with this thing in my arms!"

"Say, do you want my job?" said Hickey, scornfully, "crawling down thirty feet of air hole, with bugs, and spiders and mice? Do you? 'Cause if you do just say so."

"No-o-o," said Legs with a sigh, "no, I'll stay here."

"You don't believe in ghosts and that sort of thing, do you?" said Macnooder solicitously.

"Course, I don't!"

"All right then, 'cause if you do we won't leave you."

"You chaps go on," said Legs bravely, "only be quick about it."

" All right? "

"All right."

Hickey and Macnooder stole away; then suddenly Hickey, returning, whispered:

" Say, Legs! "

" What? "

" If you catch your coat don't think it's the dead man's hand grabbing you, will you? "

" Darn you, Hickey," said Legs, " if you don't shut up I'll quit."

" Sh-h—good-bye, old man."

" Hurry up! "

In the crawling, howling darkness Legs waited, holding the skeleton at arm's length, trembling like a leaf, listening tensely for a sound, vowing that if he ever got safely back into his bed he would never break another law of the school. At the moment when his courage was wavering, he heard the muffled, slipping tread of Macnooder returning. He drew a long comfortable breath, threw one leg nonchalantly over the back of a near-by seat and clasped the skeleton in an affectionate embrace.

" Hist—Legs."

The lantern flashed upon him. Legs yawned a bored, tranquil yawn.

"Is that you, Doc?"

"Were you scared?"

"Of what!"

"Say, you've got nerve for a youngster," said Macnooder admiringly. "Honestly, how did it feel hugging old Bonesy, all alone there in the dark?"

"You know, I rather liked it," said Legs with a drawl. "I tried to imagine what it would be like to see a ghost. Only, I could hardly keep awake. Good Lord! what's that?"

The coil of rope descending had brushed against his face and the start which he gave completely destroyed the effect of his narrative. Macnooder, seizing the rope, made it fast to the skeleton. Then, producing a large pasteboard from under his sweater, he attached it to a foot so that it would display to the morrow's audience the inscription, TABBY.

He gave two quick tugs, and the skeleton slowly ascended, twisting and turning in unnatural, white gyrations, throwing grotesque shadows against the ceiling.

`" Now, let's get up to see Hickey come out," said Macnooder with a chuckle. "He's a sight."

Ten minutes later, as they waited expectantly, listening at the opening of the narrow passage, a sneeze resounded.

"What's that?" exclaimed Legs, whose nerves were tense.

"That's Hickey," said Macnooder with a chuckle. "He'll be along in a minute. He's scattering red pepper after him so no one can crawl in to get the skeleton down. Gee! he must have swallowed half of it."

A succession of sneezes resounded, and then with a scramble an unrecognisable form shot out of the opening, covered with cobwebs and the accumulated dust of years.

"For heaven's sake, Hickey, stop sneezing!" cried Macnooder in tremor. "You'll get us pinched."

`" I—I—can't help it," returned Hickey between sneezes. "Great idea of yours—red pepper!"

"Just think of the fellow that goes in after you," said Macnooder, "and stop sneezing."

"It's in my eyes, down my throat, everywhere!" said Hickey helplessly.

They got him out of the building and down by

the pond where he plunged his head gratefully into the cooling waters. Then they slapped the dust from him and rubbed the cobwebs out of his hair, until he begged for mercy.

"Never mind, Hickey," said Macnooder helpfully, "just think of Tabby when he comes in to-morrow."

Fortified by this delicious thought, Hickey submitted to being cleaned. Then Macnooder examined him carefully, saying:

"There mustn't be the slightest clue; if there is a button missing you'll have to go back for it." Suddenly he stopped. "Hickey, there's one gone— off the left sleeve."

"I lost that scrapping with the Egghead last week," explained Hickey, "and both of the left suspender ones are gone, too."

"Honest?"

"I swear it."

"There's been many a murder tracked down," said Macnooder impressively, "on just a little button."

"Gee! Doc," said Legs in chilled admiration, "say, what a bully criminal you would make."

And on this spontaneous expression of young ambition, the three separated.

The next morning, when the school filed in to Memorial for chapel, they beheld with rapture the uncanny figure suspended directly over the rostrum. In an instant the name was whispered over the benches —"Tabby." It was then a feat of the Dickinson House. Every Dickinsonian was questioned excitedly and professed the blankest ignorance, but with such an insistent air, that twenty were instantly credited with the deed. Then, with a common impulse, the school turned to watch the entrance of the faculty. Each master on entering started, repressed an involuntary smile, looked to see the name attached, frowned, gazed fiercely at the nearest boys and took his seat.

Suddenly a thrill of excitement ran over the school and like a huge sigh the exclamation welled up, " Tabby! "

Mr. Lorenzo Blackstone Tapping had entered. His eyes met the skeleton and he coloured. A smile would have saved him, but the young Greek and Latin expert understood nothing of the humanising sciences. He tried to look unconcerned and failed; he tried to look dignified and appeared sheepish; he tried to appear calm and became red with anger. It was a moment that carried joy into the heart of Hickey, joy and the forgetfulness of red pepper, cobwebs and dust.

Then the head master arrived and a frightened calm fell over the awed assemblage. Did he see the skeleton? There was not the slightest evidence of recognition. He walked to his seat without a break and began the services without once lifting his eyes. The school was vexed, mystified and apprehensive. But at the close of the services the head master spoke, seeking the culprits among the four hundred, and under that terrifying glance each innocent boy looked guilty.

Such an outrage had never before occurred in the history of the institution, he assured them. Not only had a gross desecration been done to the sacredness of the spot, but wanton and cowardly insult had been perpetrated on one of the masters (Tapping thought the specific allusion might have been omitted). It was as cowardly as the miserable wretch who writes an anonymous letter, as cowardly as the drunken bully who shoots from the dark. He repelled the thought that this was a manifestation of the spirit of the school; it was rather the isolated act of misguided unfortunates who should never have entered the institution, who would leave it the day of their detection. And he promised the school that they would be detected, that he would neither rest nor spare an effort to ferret out this cancer and remove it.

Hickey drank in the terrific onslaught with delight. He had struck the enemy, he had made it wince and cry out. The first battle was his. He rose with the school and shuffled up the aisle. Suddenly at the exit, he beheld Mr. Tapping waiting. Their glances met in a long hostile clash. There was no mistaking the master's meaning; it was a direct accusation that sought in Hickey's face to surprise a telltale look.

A great lump rose in Hickey's throat; all the joy of a moment ago passed, a profound melancholy enveloped him; he felt alone, horribly alone, fighting against the impossible.

"Why?" he said, bitterly, "why should he always pick on me—the sneak!"

During the next few days a few minor skirmishes ensued which showed only too clearly to Hickey, the implacable persecution he must expect from Tabby. The first day it was the question of breakfast.

At seven o'clock every morning the rising bell fills

the air with its clamour from the belfry of the old gymnasium, but no one rises. There is half an hour until the gong sounds for breakfast, a long delicious half hour—the best half hour of the day or night to prolong under the covers. After twenty minutes a few effeminate members rise to prink, five minutes later there is a general tumbling out of the bed and a wild scamper into garments arranged in ingenious time-saving combinations.

At exactly the half hour, with the first sounds of the breakfast gong, Hickey would start from his warm bed, plunge his head into the already filled basin, wash with circumspection in eight seconds (drying included), thrust his legs into an arrangement of trousers, socks and unmentionables, pull a jersey over his head, stick his feet into the waiting pair of slippers, part and brush his hair, snap a " dickey " about his neck, and run down the stairs struggling into his coat, tying his tie and attending to the buttons, the whole process varying between twenty-one and one-eighth seconds and twenty-two and three-quarters.

But on the morning after the exposing of the skeleton Hickey had trouble with the dickey. The school regulations tyrannically demanded that each boy should appear at breakfast and chapel properly dressed, *i. e.,* in collar and shirt. But as the appearance is accepted for the fact, the " dickey " comes to the rescue and permits not only despatch in dressing, but by suppressing a luxury from the wash list, to attend to the necessities of the stomach. The dickey is formed by the junction of two flat cuffs, held together by a stud, to which is attached a collar, and later a tie. When the coat is added even the most practised eye may be deceived by the inclosed exhibition of linen.

On the aforesaid morning as Hickey hastily donned his dickey the stud snapped and he was forced to waste precious seconds in not only procuring another stud, but in arranging the component parts. He tore down the stairs to find the door shut in his face,—Tabby's orders, of course!

The next night the same malignant enemy surprised him at ten o'clock returning on tiptoe from the Egghead's room,—marks and penal service on Saturday afternoon. Hickey soon perceived that he was to be subjected to a constant surveillance, that the slightest absence from his room after dark would expose him to detection and punishment. Macnooder counselled seeming submission and a certain interval of patient caution. Hickey indignantly repelled the advice; the more the danger the greater the glory.

On Friday morning a strange calm pervaded the school, a lethargy universal and sweet. Seven o'clock, half past seven, a quarter of eight, and not a stir. Then suddenly in every house, exclamations of amazement burst from the rooms, watches were scanned incredulously and excited boys called from house to house. Gradually the wonder dawned, welcomed by cries of rejoicing—the clapper had been stolen!

In the Dickinson, Hickey and Macnooder were the first in the halls, the loudest in their questions, the most dumfounded at the occurrence. Breakfast, forty minutes late, was eaten in a buzz of excitement, interrupted by the arrival of a messenger from the head master with peremptory orders to convene at once in Memorial.

The Doctor was in no pleasant mood. The theft of the clapper, coming so soon upon the incident of the skeleton, had roused his fighting blood. His discourse was terse, to the point, and uncompromising. There could no longer be any doubt that individuals were in rebellion against the peace and discipline of the school. He would accept the defiance. If it was to be war, war it should be. It was for the majority to say how long they, the law-abiding, the studious, the decent, would suffer from the reckless outrages of a few without standards or seriousness of purpose. The clapper would not be replaced. All marks for tardiness and absence from recitations would be doubled, and the moment any total reached twenty, that boy would be immediately suspended from the institution. The clapper would not be replaced until the school itself replaced it!

Hickey drank in the sweet discourse, revelling in the buzz of conjecture that rose about him, concentrating all his powers on appearing innocent and unconcerned before the fusillade of admiring, alluring glances that spontaneously sought him out.

The school went to the recitation rooms joyfully, discussing how best to draw from the ultimatum all the amusement possible. By the afternoon every boy was armed with an alarm clock, which he carried into each recitation, placing it in the aisle at his feet after a solicitous comparison of the time with his neighbours. Five minutes before the close of the hour the bombardment would begin, and as each

clock exploded the owner would grab it up frantic-
ally and depart for the next recitation in a gallop.
Bright happy days, when even the monotony of the
classroom disappeared under the expectation of a
sudden alarm!

With a perfect simulation of seriousness, expedi-
tions, known as clapper parties, were organised to
search for the missing clapper. Orchards, gardens,
streams,—nothing was spared in the search. Com-
plaints began to pour in from neighbouring farmers
with threats of defending their property with shot-
guns. The school gardener arrived in a panic to
implore protection for his lawns. Then the alarm
clocks became strangely unreliable. At every moment the sound of the alarm, singly, or in bunches,
was heard in the halls of Memorial. Several of the
older members of the faculty, who were addicted to
insomnia and nervous indigestion, sent in their ultimatum. Thus forced to a decision, the head master
compromised. He had the clapper replaced and
assessed the school for the costs.

During those glorious, turbulent days, Hickey
perceived with melancholy that Tabby still persisted
in suspecting him. It was disheartening, but there
was no blinking the fact. Tabby suspected him!

At the table Tabby's eyes restlessly returned again and again in his direction. Tabby's ears were strained to catch the slightest word he might utter, in fact, everything in Tabby's bearing indicated a malignant determination to see in him the author of every escapade. This fresh injustice roused Hickey's ire to such an extent that despite the cautious Macnooder he determined upon a further deed of bravado.

One morning Mr. Lorenzo Blackstone Tapping, exactly as Hickey planned, perceived a curious watch charm on Hickey's watch chain, which he soon made out to be a miniature silver clapper. Immediately suspicious, he noticed that every boy in the room was in a state of excitement. On examining them he discovered that every waistcoat was adorned with the same suspect emblem. During the day a chance remark overheard, revealed to him the fact that Hickey was selling the souvenirs at a dollar apiece. Assuredly here was an important clue. That afternoon all his doubts were answered. He was seated at his study window when his attention was attracted by a group directly beneath. Against the wall Hickey was standing, with a large box under his arm, selling souvenirs as fast as he could make change to the breathless crowd which augmented at every moment.

Meanwhile, Hickey, fully aware of his enemy's proximity, took special pains that the conversation should carry. About him the excited crowd pressed in a frantic endeavour to purchase before the store was exhausted.

To all inquiries Hickey maintained a dark secrecy.

" I'm saying nothing, fellows, nothing at all," he said with a canny smile; " it isn't wise sometimes to do much talking. The impression has somehow got around that these little ' suveneers ' are made out of the original clapper. I'm not responsible for that impression, gents, and I make no remarks thereupon. These little ' suveneers ' I hold in my hand are silver-plated—*silver-plated*, gents, and when a thing is silver-plated there must be something inside. And I further remark that these ' suveneers ' will sell for one dollar apiece only until five o'clock, that after that time they will sell at one dollar and a half, and I further remark that there are only forty-five left! " Then rattling the box he continued with simulated innocence, " Nothing but a ' suveneer,' gents, nothing guaranteed. We sell nothing under false pretences ! "

At half past four he had sold the last of a lot of two hundred and fifty amid scenes of excitement worthy of Wall Street.

At five o'clock, Hickey received a summons to Foundation House. There to his delight he found the head master in the company of Mr. Tapping.

Hickey entered with the candour of a cherub, plainly quite at loss as to the object of the summons.

"Hicks," said the head master in his solemnest tones, "you are under very grave suspicion."

"Me, sir?" said Hickey in ungrammatical astonishment.

"Hicks, it has come to my knowledge that you are selling as souvenirs bits of the clapper that was stolen from the gymnasium."

"May I ask, sir," said Hickey with indignation, "who has accused me?"

At this Mr. Tapping spoke up severely:

"I have informed the Doctor of facts which have come into my possession."

"Sir," said Hickey, addressing the head master, "Mr. Tapping has *honoured* me with his enmity for a long while. He has not even hesitated to *threaten* me. I am not surprised that he should accuse me, only I insist that he state what evidence he has for bringing this accusation."

" Doctor, allow me," said Mr. Tapping, somewhat ill at ease. Then turning to Hickey he said, with the air of a cross-examiner: " Hicks, are you or are you not selling souvenirs at one dollar apiece, in the shape of small silver clappers? "

" Certainly."

" Made out of the original clapper? "

" Certainly *not!* "

" What! " exclaimed the amazed Tapping.

" Certainly not."

" Do you mean to say that two hundred and fifty boys would have bought those souvenirs at a dollar apiece for any other reason than that they contained a bit of the stolen clapper?"

Hickey smiled proudly.

" They may have been under that impression."

" Because you told them! "

" No, sir," said Hickey with righteous anger. " You have no right, sir, to say such a thing. On the contrary, I refused to answer one way or the other. You listened this afternoon from your window and you heard exactly my answer. If you will do me the *justice*, sir, to tell the Doctor what I did say, I shall be very much obliged to you."

"Enough, Hicks," said the head master with a frown. "Answer me directly. Are these watch charms made up out of the original clapper?"

"No, sir."

The Doctor, in his turn, looked amazed.

"Come, Hicks, that is not possible," he said. "I warn you I shall trace them without any difficulty."

Then Hickey smiled, a long delicious smile of culminating triumph. Slowly he drew forth from his pocket an envelope, from which he produced a legal document.

"If you will kindly read this, sir," he said, tending it with deepest respect.

The Doctor took it, glanced curiously at Hickey, and then began to read. Presently his face relaxed, and despite a struggle a smile appeared. Then he handed the document to Mr. Tapping, who read as follows:

I, John J. Goodsell, representing the firm of White, Brown and Bangs, jewellers of Trenton, New Jersey, take oath that I have this day engaged to manufacture for William Orville Hicks of the Lawrenceville school 250 small clappers, design submitted, of iron plated with silver, and that the iron which forms the foundation comes from scrap-iron entirely furnished by us.

Sworn to in the presence of notary.

JOHN J. GOODSELL.

Attached to the document was a bill as follows:

William Orville Hicks, Dr.,

To White, Brown and Bangs.

250 silver gilt clappers, at 11c apiece.... $27.50

Received payment.

MAKING FRIENDS

"THAT was just before I licked Whitey Brown," said Lazelle, *alias* Gazelle, *alias* the Rocky Mountain Goat and the Gutter Pup. "Cracky, that was a fight!"

"How many rounds?" asked Lovely Mead, disrobing for the night.

"Eleven and a half. Knocked him to the count

in the middle of the twelfth with a left jab to the bellows," said the Gutter Pup professionally. "He weighed ten pounds more than me. Ever do any fighting?"

"Sure," said the new arrival instantly.

"How many times?"

"Oh, I can't remember."

"You don't look it."

"Why not?"

"Your complexion's too lovely; and you're only a shaver, you know."

"I'm fifteen, almost sixteen," said Lovely, bridling up and surveying his new roommate with a calculating glance. "How old are you?"

"I've been three years at Lawrenceville, freshman," said the Gutter Pup severely. "That's the difference. What's your longest fight?"

"Twenty-one rounds," said Lovely, promptly.

"Oh," said the Gutter Pup in profound disappointment. "He licked you?"

"No."

"You licked him?"

"No."

"What then?"

"They stopped us."

"Huh!"

"We had to let it go over to the next day."

"And then?"

"Then I put him out in the thirteenth."

"Yes, you did!"

"Yes, I did."

The two fiery-haired champions stood measuring each other with their glances. Lovely Mead ran his eye over the wiry arms and chest opposite him and wondered. The Gutter Pup in veteran disdain was about to remark that Lovely was a cheerful liar when the tolling of the gym bell broke in on a dangerous situation. The Gutter Pup dove into bed and, reaching for a slipper, hurled it across the room, striking the candle fair and square and plunging the room into darkness.

"I learned that trick," he said, "the year I put the Welsh Rarebit to sleep in six." He stopped and ruminated over Lovely's story of his two-day fight, and then spoke scornfully from the dark: "I never fought anybody over eleven rounds. I never *had* to."

Lovely heard and possessed his soul in patience. He was on his second day at the school, his spirit not a whit subdued, though considerably awed, by the sacred dignities of the old boys. He liked the Gutter Pup, with one reservation, and that was an instinctive antagonism for which there was no logical explanation. But at the first fistic reminiscence of the Gutter Pup he had sought in his soul anxiously and asked himself, " Can I lick him? " Each time the question repeated itself he felt an overwhelming impulse to throw down the gage and settle the awful doubt then and there. It was pure instinct, nothing more. The Gutter Pup was really a good sort and had adopted him in quite a decent way without taking an undue advantage. In fact, Lovely was certain that in his roommate he had met the congenial soul, the chum, the best friend among all friends for whom he had waited and yearned. His heart went out to the joyous, friendly Gazelle, but his fingers contracted convulsively. Theirs was to be an enduring friendship, a sacred, Three Musketeer sort of friendship—after one small detail was settled.

The next morning Lovely Mead bounded up with the rising bell and started nervously to dress. There was a lazy commotion in the opposite bed, and then, after a few languid movements of the covers, the Gutter Pup's reddish head appeared in surprise.

"Why, Lovely, what are you doing?"

"Dressing. Didn't you hear the bell?"

"Jimminy crickets, what a waste, what an awful waste of time," said the Gutter Pup, luxuriously, stretching his arms and yawning. "Say, Lovely, I like you. You're a good sort and that was a rattlin' plucky tackle you made yesterday. Say, we're going to get on famously together, only, Lovely, you *are* green, you know."

"I suppose I am."

"You are. Of course, you can't help it, you know. Every one starts that way. Lordy, Lovely, you remind me of the first time I hit this old place, three weeks after I fought Mucker Dennis, of the Seventy-second Street gang."

Lovely Mead's gorge swelled up with indignation. To hide his emotion, he plunged his head into the basin and emerged dripping.

"I say, Lovely, I must give you some pointers," said the Gutter Pup affably. "Everything depends, you know, on the start. You want to stand in with the masters, you know. Study hard the first week and get your lessons down fine, and work up their weak points, and you'll slide through the term with ease and pleasure."

" What are these weak points? " inquired Lovely from the depths of a clean shirt.

" Oh, I mean the side they're most approachable. Now the Roman, you know, when he makes a joke you always want to laugh as though you were going to die."

" Does he make many jokes? " asked Lovely.

" Cracky, yes. Then there's one very important one he makes around Thanksgiving that every one watches for. I'll put you on, but you must be very careful."

" What? The same joke every year? " said Lovely.

" Regular. It's about Volturcius in Cæsar—the ' c ' is soft, you know, but you have to pronounce it —Vol-turk-ious."

" Why so? "

" So the Roman can say, ' No-o, no-o, not even the near approach of Thanksgiving will justify such a pronunciation.' See? That's the cue to laugh until the tears wet the page. It's most important."

" What about the Doctor? "

" Easy, dead easy; just ask questions, side-path questions that'll lead him away from the lesson and give him a chance to discourse. Say—another thing, Lovely, don't go and buy anything in the village; let me do that for you."

" Thanks."

" I'm on to their games, you know; I'm wise. Oh, say, another pointer—about the jigger-shop. You want to build up your credit with Al, you know."

" How d'you mean? "

" The best way is to get trusted right off while you've got the chink and then pay up promptly at the end of a week, and repeat the operation a couple of times. Then Al thinks you're conscientious about debts and that sort of thing, and when the hard-up months come he'll let you go the limit."

" I say, Lazelle," said Lovely, admiringly, " you've got it down pretty fine, haven't you? It's real white of you to look after me this way."

" You're all right," said the Gutter Pup, still lolling in bed. " All you want is to lay low for a month or so and no one'll bother you. Besides, I'll see to that."

" Thank you."

" You see, Lovely, I've taken a fancy to you: a real, live, fat, young fancy. You remind me of Bozy Walker that was fired for introducing geese into the Muffin Head's bedroom; dear old Bozy, he stood up to me for seven rounds."

Lovely Mead dropped the hairbrush in his agitation and drew a long breath. How much longer could his weak human nature hold out? Downstairs the gong began to call them to breakfast. With the first sound the Gutter Pup was in the middle of the floor, out of his pajamas and into his clothes before the gong had ceased to ring. He plunged his head into the basin already filled with water, dried himself, parted the moist hair with one sweeping stroke of his comb, snapped a dickey about his neck and struggled into his coat while Lovely was still staring with amazement.

" That's the way it's done," said the Gutter Pup, triumphantly. " There's only one fellow in the school can beat me out, and that's that old Hickey, over in the Dickinson; but I'll beat him yet. Are you ready? Come on! "

The trouble was that the Gutter Pup was absolutely unaware of the disturbance in Lovely's mind, or that his reminiscences provoked such thoughts of combat. He took Lovely to the village and fitted him out, hectoring the tradesmen and smashing prices with debonair impudence that Lovely sneak-

ingly envied. Certainly the Gutter Pup was unusually cordial and did not in the least make him
feel the indignities of his position of newcomer, as
he had a right to do.

After supper they worked on the arrangement of
their room. The Gutter Pup grew ecstatic as
Lovely produced his treasures from the bottom of
the trunk.

"My aunt's cat's kittens!" he ejaculated as
Lovely produced a set of pennants in gaudy ar-
rangement. "Will we have the boss room, though!
Lovely, you are a treasure! This will make the
Waladoo Bird turn pale and weep for sorrow. Sup-
posin' we ruminate."

They ranged their accumulated possessions on the
floor, and sat back to consider.

"Well," said the Gutter Pup, "let's begin by putting the cushions on the window-seat and the rugs
on the floor. Now the question is—what's to have
the place of honour?"

"What have you got?" asked Lovely, considering.

"I've got a signed photograph of John L. Sulli-
van," said the Gutter Pup, proudly producing it.
"It used to be cleaner, but Butsey White blew up
with a root-beer bottle and spattered it."

"Is it his own signature?" inquired Lovely, gazing in awe.

"Sure. Dear old John L. He *was* a fighter. Now, what have *you* got?"

"I've got a picture of an actress."

"Honest?"

"Sure."

"Who is it?"

"Maude Adams."

"You don't say so!"

"Fact."

"It isn't signed, Lovely—it can't be?"

"It is."

"Cracky! That *is* a prize. Maude Adams! Think of it! What will the Waladoo Bird say?"

The Gutter Pup gazed reverently at the priceless photograph and said in a breath:

"Maude Adams and John L.; think of it, Lovely!" He paused and added in a burst of gratitude: "Say, you can call me Gazelle or Razzle-dazzle now, if you want; afterward we'll see about Gutter Pup."

Lovely was too overcome by this advance to voice his feelings, but his heart went out to his new friend, all irritation forgotten. After long discussion it was decided that the two photographs, being of unique and equal value, should be hung side by side on the background of an American flag. The pennants were strung as a border around the walls, but were speedily hidden under an imposing procession of light-weight and middle-weight champions, sporting prints, posters and lithographic reproductions of comic opera favourites, boxing gloves, fencing masks, lacrosse sticks, Japanese swords, bird nests, stolen signs, photographs of athletic teams, cotillon favours and emblems of the school and the Woodhull. They stopped and gazed in awe and admiration, and falling gleefully into each other's arms, executed a dance about the room. Then Lovely Mead, in an unthinking moment, standing before the photograph of the mighty John L., exclaimed: " Say, Gazelle, isn't he a wonder, though! How long have you had it? "

" I got it," said the Gutter Pup, putting his head on one side and reflecting, " right after I fought Whitey Brown—just before my mill with Doggie Shephard—a year and a half ago, I should say."

All the joy of the home-building left Lovely. He sat down on the bed and pulled at his shoestrings so viciously that they broke off in his hand.

" What's the matter? " said the Gutter Pup in surprise.

" Nothing."

" You look sort-of put out."

" Oh, no."

" Whitey was a tough one," resumed the Gutter Pup, lolling on the window-seat, " but Doggie was no great shakes. Too fat and overgrown. He did look big, but he had no footwork and his wind was bad—very bad."

Lovely Mead listened with averted eyes.

If he had only been an old boy he would have thrown down the gauntlet then and there; but he was a freshman and must check the tugging within. Besides, there must be some excuse. He could not openly, out of clear sky, provoke an old boy who had taken him under his protection and had done everything to make him feel at home. Such an act would be fresh, and would bring down on him the condemnation of the whole school.

" Why the deuce should I care, after all?" he asked himself gloomily that night. " What difference does it make how many fellows he's licked. I suppose it's because I'm a coward. That's it; it's because I'm afraid that he would lick me that it rankles so. Am I a coward, after all, I wonder?"

This internal questioning became an obsession. It

clouded his days and took the edges from the keen joy of romping over the football field and earning the good word of Tough McCarthy for his neat diving tackles. Could the Gutter Pup lick him, after all? He wondered, he debated, he doubted. He began to brood over it until he became perfectly unapproachable, and the Gutter Pup, without a suspicion of the real cause, began to assure Hasbrouck that Lovely was being overtrained.

Meanwhile, matters were approaching a crisis with Lovely. Each morning he calculated the strength of the Gutter Pup's chest and arms, and wondered what was the staying power of his legs. Sometimes he admitted to himself that he wouldn't last three rounds. At others he figured out a whole plan of campaign that must wear down the Gutter Pup and send him to a crashing defeat. Waking, he went through imaginary rounds, received without wincing tremendous, imaginary blows, and sent in sledge-hammer replies that inevitably landed the champion prone on his back. At night his dreams were a long conglomeration of tussling and battle in the most unexpected places. He fought the Gutter Pup at the top of the water-tower and saw him vanish over the edge as the result of a smashing blow on the point of the jaw; he fought him on the football field and in the classroom, while the Roman held the watch and the head master insisted on refereeing.

The worst of it was, he knew he was going to pieces and moping in a way to render himself a nuisance to all his associates; and yet he couldn't help it. Try as he would to skip the mention of any subject that could be tagged to a date, every now and then an opening would come, and the Gutter Pup would begin: "Let me see; that must have been just after I fought——"

At last, one night, unable to bear the strain longer, Lovely went to his room resolved to end it. He bided his opportunity, gazing with unseeing eyes at the pages of the divine Virgil. Finally he raised his head and said, abruptly: "Say, Lazelle, what do you think of our chances for the football championship?"

"Fair, only fair," said the Gutter, glad for any excuse to stop studying. "The Davis and the Dickinson look better to me."

"How long has it been since we won?" said Lovely, scarcely breathing.

"Let me see," said the Gutter Pup, unsuspecting.

" We won the fall I fought Legs Brownell behind the Davis house."

" Lazelle," said Lovely, rising desperately, " I can lick you ! "

" What ? "

" I can lick you ! "

" Hello," said the Gutter Pup, considering him in amazement; " what does this mean ? "

" It means I can lick you," repeated Lovely doggedly, advancing and clenching his fists.

" You want a fight ? "

" I do."

" Why, bully for you ! "

The Gutter Pup considered, joyfully, with a glance at the clock.

" It's too late now to pull it off. We'll let it go until to-morrow night. Besides, you'll be in better condition then, and you can watch your food, which is important. I'll notify Hickey. You don't mind fighting by lamplight ? "

" Huh ! "

" Of course, we'll fight under the auspices of the Sporting Club, with a ring and sponges and that sort of thing," said the Gutter Pup cheerfully. " You'll like it. It's a secret organisation and it's a great honour to belong. Hickey, at the Dickinson, got it up. He's president, and referees. I'm the official timekeeper, but that don't matter. They'll arrange for seconds and all that sort of thing, and Doc Macnooder is always there for medical assistance. You're sure the lights won't bother you?"

" No."

" It's a queer effect, though. First time I fought Snapper Bell——"

" Lazelle," said Lovely, choking with rage, " I can lick you, right now—here—and I don't believe you ever licked anyone in your life!"

" Look here, freshman," said the Gutter Pup, at once on his dignity; " I've stood enough of your impertinence. You'll do just as I say, and you'll act like a gentleman and a sport and not like a member of the Seventy-second Street gang. We'll fight like sportsmen, to-morrow, at midnight, under the auspices of the Sporting Club, in the baseball cage, and until then I'll dispense with your conversation! Do you hear me?"

Lovely Mead felt the justice of the reproof. Yes, he *had* acted like a member of the Seventy-second Street gang! He glanced up at the photograph (slightly spotted) of John L., and he thought of

Ivanhoe and the Three Musketeers, and Sir Nigel of the White Company, and presently he said, tentatively:

" I say——"

No answer.

" Lazelle——"

Still no answer.

" Say, I want to—to apologise. You're right about the Seventy-second Street gang. I'm sorry."

" All right," said the Gutter Pup, not quite appeased. " I'm glad you apologised."

" But we fight to-morrow—to the end—to the limit ! "

" You're on ! "

They spoke no more that night, undressing in silence, each covertly swelling his muscles and glancing with stolen looks at his opponent's knotted torso. By morning the Gutter Pup's serenity had returned.

" Well, how're you feeling? How did you sleep? " he asked, poking his nose over the coverlets.

" Like a log," returned Lovely, lying gloriously.

" Good. Better take a nap in the afternoon, though, if you're not used to midnight scrapping."

" Thanks."

"Mind the food—no hot biscuits, and that sort of thing. A dish of popovers almost put me to the bad the first time I met Bull Dunham. Fact, and he didn't know enough to counter."

Lovely dressed and hurriedly left the room.

At two o'clock, to his amazement, Charley De Soto, the great quarterback, in person, waited on him in company with the gigantic Turkey Reiter, tackle on the eleven, and informed him that they had been appointed his seconds and anxiously inquired after his welfare.

"I—oh, I'm doing pretty well, thank you, sir," said Lovely, overcome with embarrassment and pride.

"Say, Charley," said Turkey, after an approving examination, "I kind of hanker to the looks of this here bantam. He's got the proper colour hair and the protruding jaw. Danged if I don't believe he'll give the Gutter Pup the fight of his life."

"Can you lick him?" said De Soto, looking Lovely tensely in the eyes.

"I'll do it or die," said Lovely, with a lump in his throat.

"Good, but mind this, youngster: no funking. I don't stand second to any quitter. If I'm behind you, you've *got* to win."

Lovely thought at that moment that death on the rack would be a delight if it only could win a nod of approbation from Charley De Soto.

"How's your muscles?" asked Turkey. He ran his fingers over him, slapped his chest and punched his hips, saying:

"Hard as a rock, Charley."

"How's your wind?" said De Soto.

"Pretty well, thank you, sir," said Lovely, quite overcome by the august presence.

"Now keep your mind off things. Don't let the Gutter Pup bluff you. Slip over to the Upper, right after lights, and I'll take charge of the rest. By the way, Turk, who's in the corner with the Gutter Pup?"

"Billy Condit and the Triumphant Egghead."

"Good. We'll just saunter over and lay a little bet. So-long, youngster. No jiggers or éclairs. See you later."

"So-long, old Sporting Life," added Turkey, with a friendly tap on the shoulder. "Mind now, keep cheerful."

Lovely's mood was not exactly cheerful. In fact he felt as if the bottom had fallen out of things. He tried his best to follow Charley De Soto's advice and not think of the coming encounter, but, do what he would, his mind slipped ahead to the crowded baseball cage, the small, ill-lighted ring, and the Gutter Pup.

"After all, will he lick me?" he said, almost aloud. His heart sank, or rather it was a depression in the pit of his stomach.

"Supposing he does?" he went on, pressing his knuckles against his teeth. What a humiliation after his boast! There would be only one thing to do— leave school at once, and never, never return!

He had wandered down to the football field where the candidates for the school eleven were passing and falling on the ball under the shouted directions of the veterans. The bulky figure of Turkey Reiter, gigantic with its padded shoulders and voluminous sweater, hove into view, and the tackle's rumbling voice cried out:

"Hi there, old Sockarooster, this won't do! Keep a-laughin'; keep cheerful; tumble down here and shag for me."

Lovely Mead went gratefully to fetch the balls that Turkey booted, far down the field, to the waiting halfbacks.

"Feeling a bit serious, eh?" said Turkey.

" Well——"

" Sure you are. That's nothing. Don't let the Gutter Pup see it, though. He's got to believe we are holding you in, chaining you up, keepin' you under the bars, 'cause you're barking to get at him. Savvy? Chuck in a bluff, old sport, and—keep cheerful. Better now? "

" Yes, thank you," said Lovely, who was in nowise suffering from an excess of hilarity.

He did not see the Gutter Pup until supper, and then had to undergo again his solicitous inquiries. By a horrible effort he succeeded in telling a funny story at the table, and laughed until his own voice alarmed him. Then he relapsed into silence, smiling furiously at every remark, and chewing endlessly on food that had no flavour for him.

"Lovely," said the Gutter Pup upstairs, shaking his head, " you don't look fit; you're getting nervous."

" Sure," said Lovely, remembering Turkey's injunction. " I'm a high-strung, *vicious* temperaament ! "

" Your eye acts sort of loose," said the Gutter Pup, unconvinced. " You're new to fighting before a big assemblage. It's no wonder. I don't want any *accidental* advantages. Say the word and we'll put it over."

"No," said Lovely, quite upset by his friendly offer. "I only hope, Lazelle, I can hold myself in. I've got an awful temper; I'm afraid I'll kill a man some day."

"No, Lovely," said Gutter Pup, shaking his head. "You don't deceive me. You are ill—ill, I tell you, and you might as well own up."

The truth was, Lovely was ill and rapidly getting worse under the insouciance of the veteran of the ring.

"Why, my aunt's cat's pants, Lovely," said the Gutter Pup seriously. "That's nothing to be ashamed of. Didn't I get it the same way the first time I went up against Bloody Davis, of the Murray Hill gang, on a bet I'd stick out three rounds?"

Lovely Mead drew a sigh of relief. The red blood seemed to rush back into his veins once more, and his lungs to resume their appointed functions.

"September's a good month for these little things," he said hopefully.

"October's better, more snap in the air," said the Gutter Pup. "September's muggy. I remember when I was matched against Slugger Kelly; it was so hot I lost ten pounds, and the fight only went five rounds, at that.'

The old provocation had roused up the old antagonism in Lovely. He hardly dared trust himself longer in the room, so he bolted and slipped down to the Waladoo's room and out into the campus.

" Gee," he said to himself, with a sigh of relief, " if I could only get at him *now!* "

At taps he went cautiously to the Upper, by the back way, and gained the room of Charley De Soto, where he was told to turn in on the window-seat and take it easy.

Presently Turkey Reiter and Macnooder arrived to discuss the probabilities. Then Bojo Lowry, who could play anything, sat down at the piano and performed the most wonderful variations and medleys, until Lovely forgot any future engagement in the delight of gazing from his cushioned recess on real Fourth Formers, enjoying the perquisites and liberties of the Upper House.

Suddenly Macnooder glanced at his watch and announced that it was almost midnight. Lovely sprang up feverishly.

" Here, young Sporting Life," cried Turkey, " no

champing on the bit! Just a dash of calm and tranquillity."

"Easy, easy there," said De Soto, with a professional glance.

"Ready here," said Macnooder, picking up a
brown satchel. "I'll bleed him if he faints."

They separated, and, on tiptoe, by various routes,
departed from the Upper, making wide circles in the
darkness before seeking the baseball cage, Lovely
Mead supported on either side by Charley De Soto
and Turkey.

They gave the countersign at the door, and were
admitted noiselessly into the utter blackness of the
baseball cage. Lovely waited in awe, unable to distinguish anything, clutching at Turkey's arm.

"Is the Gutter Pup here yet?" said De Soto's
voice, in a whisper.

Another voice, equally guarded, replied: "Just
in."

From time to time the door opened on the starry
night and vague forms flitted in. Then other voices
spoke:

"What time is it?"

"Midnight, Hickey."

"Lock the door; no admittance now. Egghead, show up with the light. Strike up, Morning Glory!"

A bull's-eye flashed out from one corner, and then two lanterns filled the gloom with their trembling flicker.

Out of the mist suddenly sprang forty-odd members of the Sporting Club, grouped about a vacant square in the middle of the cage which had been roped off. De Soto and Turkey pushed forward to their appointed stations, where chairs had been placed for the principals. Lovely seated himself and glanced across the ropes. The Gutter Pup was already in his corner, stripped to the waist, and being gently massaged by the Triumphant Egghead and Billy Condit, captain of the eleven.

In the middle of the ring, Hickey, in his quality of president and referee, was giving his directions in low, quick syllables. The assembled sporting gentlemen pressed forward for the advantage of position; the two front ranks assuming sitting or crouching positions, over which the back rows craned. Lovely gazed in awe at the select assembly. The élite of the school was there. He saw Glendenning, Rock Bemis and Tough McCarthy of his own house, scattered among such celebrities as Crazy Opdyke, the Mugwump Politician, Goat Phillips, who ate the necktie, and the Duke of Bilgewater, Wash Simmons, Cap Kiefer, Stonewall Jackson, Tug Moffat, Slugger Jones, Ginger-Pop Rooker, Cheyenne Baxter, Red Dog, Hungry Smeed, and Beauty Sawtelle, all silently estimating the strength of the freshman who had to go up against the veteran Gutter Pup.

Referee Hickey paid a quick visit to the contending camps, and was assured that each antagonist was restrained from flying at his opponent's throat only by the combined efforts of his seconds.

"Gentlemen of the Sporting Club," said Hickey, scraping one foot and shooting his collar, as referees do, "Before proceeding with the evening's entertainment, the management begs to remind you that the labours incident to the opening of the school have been unusually heavy—unusually so; and, as we particularly desire that nothing shall be done to disturb the slumbers of our overworked Faculty, we will ask you to applaud only in the English fashion, by whispering to your neighbour, 'Oh, very well struck, indeed,' when you are moved to excitement. We gently remind you that any one breaking forth into cheers will be first slugged and then expelled.

"Gentlemen of the Sporting Club, I have the

honour to present to you the evening's contestants. On the right, our well-known sporting authority, Mr. Gutter Pup Lazelle, known professionally as the Crouching Kangaroo.   On the left, Mr. Lovely Mead, the dark horse from Erie, Pennsylvania, who has been specially fed on raw beef in preparation for the encounter.   Both boys are members of the Wood-hull branch of this club.   The rounds will be of three minutes each—one minute intermission.   Mr. Welsh Rabbit Simpson will act as timekeeper, and will return the stop-watch *immediately* on conclusion of the exercises.   Both contestants have signified their desire to abide strictly to the rules laid down by the late Marquess of Queensberry, bless him!   No fouls will be tolerated, and only one blow may be struck in the break-away.

" In the corner for the Gutter Pup, Mr. William Condit, the tiddledy-winks champion, and the only Triumphant Egghead in captivity.

" In the corner for Lovely, Mr. Turkey Reiter, the Dickinson Mud Lark, and Mr. Charles De Soto, the famous crochet expert.   Doctor Macnooder, the Trenton veterinary, is in attendance, but will *not* be allowed to practice.   The referee of the evening will be that upright and popular sportsman, the Honourable Hickey Hicks. Let the contestants step into the ring."

Lovely was shoved to his feet and propelled forward by a resounding slap on his shoulders from Turkey Reiter. He had sat in a daze, awed by the strange, imposing countenances of the school celebrities, duly submitting to the invigorating massage of his seconds, hearing nothing of the directions showered on him. Now he was actually in the ring, feeling the hard earth under his feet, looking into the eyes of the Gutter Pup, who came up cheerfully extending his hand. Surprised, Lovely took it, and grinned a sheepish grin.

"Ready—go!" came the command.

Instantly the Gutter Pup sprang back, assuming that low, protective attitude which had earned from Hickey the epithet of the Crouching Kangaroo. Lovely, very much embarrassed, extended his left arm, holding his right in readiness while he moved mechanically forward on the point of his toes. The Gutter Pup, smiling at him, churned his arms and shifted slightly to one side. Strangely enough, Lovely felt all his resentment vanish. He no longer had the slightest desire to hurl himself on his antagonist. Indeed, it would at that moment have seemed quite a natural act to extend his hand to the joyful Gutter Pup and close the incident with a laugh. But there he was, irrevocably destined to fight before the assembled Sporting Club, under penalty of everlasting disgrace. He made a tentative jab and sprang lightly back from the Gutter Pup's reply. Then he moved forward and backward, feinting with his left and right, wishing all the time that the Gutter Pup would rush in and strike him, that he might attack with anger instead of this weakening mental attitude to which he was at present a prisoner. Twice the Gutter Pup's blows grazed his head, and once landed lightly on his chest, without his being at all moved from his calm. The call of " Time " surprised him. He went to his seconds frowning.

"What's wrong, young'n? " said De Soto. " You're not in the game."

" No," said Lovely, shaking his head. " I—I've got to get mad first."

" All right, that'll come. Keep cool and play to tire him out," said De Soto, satisfied. " Make him do the prancing around; don't you waste any energy."

" Time! " whispered the Welsh Rabbit.

Again he was in the ring, experiencing once more
that same incomprehensible feeling of sympathy for
the Gutter Pup. The more he danced about, shaking
his head and feinting with quick, nervous jabs, the
more Lovely's heart warmed up to him. Wasn't he
a jolly, genial chap, though? Desperately Lovely
strove to remember some fault, a word or a look that
had once offended him. In vain; nothing came. He
liked the chap better than he had ever liked any one
before. He struck out as one strikes at his dearest
friend, and a low groan of disgust rose from the
Sporting Club.

"Ah, put some steam in it!"

"Do you think you're pickin' cherries?"

"That's it—be polite!"

"Sister, don't hurt little brother!"

The Welsh Rabbit spoke:

"Time!"

Not a real blow had yet been struck. Lovely went
to his corner perplexed.

"That's the boy," said De Soto, with a satisfied
shake of his head. "That's the game! Don't mind
what you hear. Play the long game. The Crouching Kangaroo style is all very pretty, but it doesn't
save the wind."

"Never mind the ballet steps, Sport," added Turkey, vigorously applying the towel. "Hold in, but when you do start, rip the in'ards out of things."

"They think I'm doing it on purpose," said Lovely to himself.

"Time!" called the Welsh Rabbit.

The Gutter Pup, changing his tactics, as though he had sufficiently reconnoitred, began to attack with rapid, pestiferous blows that annoyed Lovely as a swarm of gnats annoys a dog. He shook his head angrily and sought an opportunity to strike, but the fusillade continued, light but disconcerting. When he struck, the Gutter Pup slipped away or ducked and returned smiling and professional to attack. Lovely began to be irritated by the Gutter Pup's complacency. He wasn't serious enough,— his levity was insulting. Also, he was furious because the Gutter Pup would not strike him a blow that hurt. His jaw set and he started to rush.

"Time!" said the Welsh Rabbit.

Lovely went to his corner unconvinced.

"Are the rounds three minutes?" he asked.

"Sure," said Turkey. "Don't worry; they'll get longer."

Lovely looked across at the opposite camp. The

adherents of the Gutter Pup were patting him on the back, exulting over his work.

"What's he done?" said Lovely, angrily, to himself; "that sort of work wouldn't hurt a fly."

"Time!" said the Welsh Rabbit.

Lovely walked slowly to meet the Gutter Pup, bursting with irritation. He waited, and as the Gutter Pup attacked he plunged forward, taking a blow in the face, and drove his fist joyfully into the chest before him. The Gutter Pup went back like a tenpin, staggered, and kept his footing. When he came up there was no longer a smile in his eyes.

They threw boxing to the winds. It was give and take, fast and furious, back and forth against the ropes, and rolling over and over on the ground.

"Time!" announced the Welsh Rabbit, and Hickey had to pry them apart.

Lovely thought the intermission would never end. He sat stolidly, paying no heed to his seconds' prayers to go slow, to rest up this next round, to make the Gutter Pup work. He would fight his fight his own way, without assistance.

"Time!" said the Welsh Rabbit.

Lovely started from his corner for the thing that came to meet him without yielding, exchanging blows without attempt at blocking, rushing into clinches, locking against the heaving chest, looking into the strange, wild eyes, pausing for neither breath nor rest.

Once he was rushed across the ring, fighting back like a tiger, and jammed over the ropes into the ranks of the spectators. Then he caught the Gutter Pup off his balance, and drove him the same way, his arms working like pistons. The rounds continued and ended with nothing to choose between them.

Lovely felt neither the blows received nor the rough rubbing-down of his seconds. He heard nothing but the sharp cries of " Time! " and sometimes he didn't hear that; but a rough hand would seize him (was it Hickey's?) and tear him away from the body against him.

He went down several times, wondering what had caused it, quits for standing moments triumphantly, while the fallen Gutter Pup raised himself from the ground.

Then he lost track of the rounds; and the rows of sweaters and funny white faces about the ring seemed to swell and multiply into crowds that stretched far back and up. The lights seemed to be going out— getting terribly dim and unsteady.

"Then he lost track of the rounds"

Once in his corner he thought he heard some one say: "Fifteenth round"—fifteen, and he could remember only six. In fact, he had forgotten whom he was fighting or what it was about, only that some one on whose knee he was resting was shrieking in his ear:

"He's all out, Lovely. You've got him. Just one good soak—just one *lovely* one!"

That was a joke, he supposed—a poor joke—but he would see to that "one soak" the next round.

"Time!" cried the Welsh Rabbit.

For the sixteenth time the seconds raised their champions, steadied them, and sent them forth. One good blow would send either toppling over to the final count. So they craned forward in wild excitement, exhorting them in hoarse whispers.

The two contestants gyrated up and stood blankly regarding each other. About them rose a murmur of voices:

"Sail in!"

"Soak him, Lovely!"

"Clean him up, Gutter Pup!"

"One to the jaw!"

"Now's your time!"

With a simultaneous movement each raised his

right and shot it lumberingly forward, past the hazy, confronting head, fruitlessly into the air. Renewed whispers, dangerously loud, arose:

"Now's your chance, Gutter Pup!"

"Draw off and smash him!"

"He's all yours, Lovely!"

"Oh, Lovely, hit him! hit him!"

"Just once!"

They neither heard nor cared. Their arms locked lovingly about their shoulders, and they began to settle. New cries:

"Break away!"

"Don't let him pull you down!"

"Keep your feet, Lovely!"

"They're both going!"

With a gradual, deliberate motion, Lovely and the Gutter Pup sat down, still affectionately embraced; then, wavering a moment, careened over and lay blissfully unconscious. Amazement and perplexity burst forth.

"Why, they're done for!"

"They're out—they're both out!"

"Sure enough."

"What happens?"

"Who wins?"

" Well, did you ever——"

Suddenly Hickey, standing forward, began to count:

" One, two, three——"

" What's he doing that for? "

" Aren't they both down? "

" Four, five, six, seven——"

" But Lovely went first! "

" No, the Gutter Pup."

" Eight, nine, *TEN!* " cried Hickey. " I declare both men down and out. The Sporting Club will register one knockout to the credit of the Gutter Pup and one to Lovely Mead. All bets off. The Welsh Rabbit will proceed to return that watch!! "

At seven o'clock the next morning Lovely, from his delicious bed, gazed across at the swollen head of the Gutter Pup. At the same instant the Gutter Pup, opening his eyes, perceived the altered map of Lovely's features.

" Lovely," he said brokenly, " you're the finest ever. You're a man after my own heart! "

" Razzle-dazzle," replied Lovely, choking, " you're the finest sport and gentleman in the land. I love you better than a brother."

" Lovely, that was the greatest fight that has ever been fought," said the Gutter Pup. " You are *the* daisy scrapper ! "

" Razzle-dazzle——"

" Call me Gutter Pup."

" Gutter Pup, you've got the nerve market cornered."

" Lovely, I haven't felt so happy since the day I stood up five rounds——"

Suddenly the Gutter Pup stopped and added apologetically: " Say, Lovely, honest, does my au-to-biography annoy you? "

And Lovely replied happily:

" No, Gutter Pup, honest—not now."

THE HERO OF AN HOUR

GEORGE BARKER SMITH was one of the four-hundred-odd boys whose names figure in the school catalogue at the commencement of each year. He had passed from the shell into the first form, from the first form into the second, where he had remained an extra year, during the elongating, dormant period of his growth, and another year, during the dormant, elongating one. Then in the seventh year of his career he finally achieved the fourth form and entered the Upper House.

During this generous stay he had done nothing

to distinguish himself from his neighbour. He had never accomplished anything heroic, attempted anything daring, or done anything ridiculous. After seven years his record was so blank that even the fertile imaginations of Hickey and Macnooder could find nothing on which to hang a nickname. Besides, it is doubtful if they ever stopped to think of George Barker Smith. He filled in, he was the average—a part of the great background of school life, which made up the second teams in athletic contests and substituted occasionally on the banjo and mandolin clubs, after borrowing a dress suit across the hall.

He ran in debt at the jigger-shop, like everyone else, or he might have been called Miser. He flunked in Greek and mathematics sufficiently to escape the epithet of Poler. He had occasionally been read out at roll-call for absence from bath, thus invalidating the right to Soapsuds or Wash.

Sometimes, when his neighbours dropped in on him in quest of stamps or a collar or a jersey, they called him affectionately Smithy, old Sockarooster. But he was not deceived, and loaned from his wardrobe with a full comprehension of the value of endearing terms. Smithy! After seven years he was just Smithy—his whole story was there.

And in the secret places of his heart, which no boy reveals, George Barker Smith grieved. Covertly he felt his obscureness and rebelled. After seven years' afflictions he would pass from Lawrenceville and be forgotten. And all for the lack of a nickname! If Nature had only formed him so that he might have aspired to the appellation of the Triumphant Egghead. The Triumphant Egghead— that was a name to be proud of! Who could ever forget that? There was fame secure and imperishable; neither years nor distance could dim the memory!

No, Nature had not been considerate of him. His nose was just a nose, not a Beekstein; his ears were ordinary ears, not Flop Ears; his teeth were regular and all present. No one would ever call him Walrus or Tuskarora Smith, which sounds so well. He was not tall enough to be called Ladders or Beanpole; he was not small enough for Runt, Tiny, Wee-wee, or The Man. He was just average size, average weight, which barred a whole category, such as Skinny, Puff-Ball, Shanks, Slab-Sides, Jumbo, Flea, Bigboy and Razors.

To pass into the world and be forgotten! To fade from the memory of his classmates or to linger indistinctly as one of the Smiths between Charles D. and George R.! And all for the lack of a nickname! George Barker Smith, brooding thereon, envied the Gutter Pup, who likewise rejoiced in the appellation of Razzle-dazzle and the Rocky Mountains Gazelle; he envied the Waladoo Bird, the Coffee-Cooler, the Morning Glory; he envied Two-Inches Brown, whose indiscreet remark that he needed but that to make the 'varsity nine had at least enrolled his name on the list of celebrities; but most of all he envied the Triumphant Egghead. With that glorious title as model, he sought in himself for something which might reclaim him—and found nothing. From Barker Smith might be made Doggie or Bow-wow Smith, but even that lacked naturalness and application. No, there was no turning his destiny; Smithy it was decreed and Smithy it would remain.

It was not fame Smith sought. His spirit was not of the sort that drags angels down. Naturally there had been periods in his youth when he had dreamed of reaching the Homeric proportions of Turkey Reiter or Slugger Jones; of scurrying over the gridiron, darting through a maze of frantic tacklers like Flash Condit, who had scored against the Princeton 'varsity in that glorious eight to four game; of knocking out dramatic home runs like Cap Kiefer, that bring joy out of sorrow and end in towering bonfires. These are glories which all may dream of but few attain.

Neither did he ask for the gifts of a Hungry Smeed, for to possess the ability to eat forty-nine pancakes at a sitting was a talent that is not lightly bestowed. No, he did not ask for fame; all he asked was to be remembered; for some incident or accident to come which would mark him with a glorious, fantastic nickname that would live with the Triumphant Egghead and the Duke of Bilgewater. And Fate, which sometimes listens to prayers, was kind and brought him not only a nickname but fame—real enduring fame. For in the most extraordinary way it came to pass that George Barker Smith unwittingly accomplished a feat which no boy had ever dared before and which it is extremely unlikely will ever be duplicated in the future. And this is the manner in which greatness was thrust upon him.

In the last days of the month of September the school returned from the fatiguing period of vacation to seek recuperation and needed sleep in the classrooms. George Barker Smith found himself at last a full-fledged fourth former, one of the lords of the school, member of a free governing body, with license to burn the midnight lamp unchallenged, to stray into the village at all hours, to visit the jigger-shop during school and remain tranquilly seated when a master bore down from the horizon, instead of joining the palpitating under-formers that just at his back crouched, glasses in hand, behind the counter. No longer did he have to stand in file once a week before the Bursar to claim a beggarly half-dollar allowance. Instead, once a mouth he strolled in at his pleasure and nonchalantly tendered checks for fifty dollars, with which allowance his parents, for one blissful year only, fondly expected him to purchase all the clothes necessary—per agreement.

He could hire a buggy at ruinous rates and disappear in search of distant cider-mills or visit friends in Princeton, who had gone before. Finally, his room was his castle, where no imperious tapping of a lurking undermaster would come to disturb a little party at the national game, for chips only, of course.

George Barker Smith's room was on the third floor back and had attached to it certain communal rights. Even as the possession of the ground-floor

rooms in the under-form houses entailed the obliga-
tion to assist at all hours of the night the passage
to the outer world, and to assure the safe return
therefrom, so room 67 was the recognised highway
to the roof of the Upper, when the thermometer
had mounted above seventy-eight degrees Fahrenheit.

Those who sought the cooling heights sought security and (be it confessed, now that an inconsid-
erate Faculty's sanction has made smoking no longer
a pleasure but a choice) the companionship of the
Demon Cigarette or the " Coffin Nail," as it was more
affectionately known. The guardianship of this
highway, if it entailed responsibilities, also brought
with it certain perquisites and tariffs in the shape of
an invitation without expense.

Now, George Barker Smith did not like the odour
of tobacco in the least, and he particularly disliked
the effects produced by the cheap cigarette which
the price rendered popular. But once a fourth
former there were so few rules to break that this opportunity had to be embraced as an imperative duty,
and so he resigned himself, pretending (like how
many others!) to inhale and enjoy it.

The last weeks of September were unusually hot
and distressing. The stiff collar disappeared. Two-

piece suits became the fashion for full dress and fatigue uniform consisted of considerably less. The day was passed in long, grumbling siestas under the shade of apple trees or in a complete surrender to the cooling contact of peach and strawberry jiggers. Even games lost their attraction, and the only sign of life was the pleasant spectacle of the heavy squad on the football team, puffing protestingly about the circle under the cruel necessity of reducing weight.

After dark, bands were organised which stole away, through negro villages, arousing frantic dogs, to the banks of the not-too-fragrant canal, where they spent a long, blissful hour frolicking in the moonlit water or raising their voices in close harmony on the bank. Other spirits, not so adventurous, contented themselves with lining up behind the Upper in white, shivering line, where the hose brought comfort as it played over grateful backs.

Naturally, at night, smoking up the flue, even with the whispered conversations with the boy below and the boy across, lost all charm. The roof became a veritable rookery. Mattresses were carried up and hot, suffocating boys lolled through the raging night swapping yarns and gazing at the inscrutable stars. On a certain evening, hot among the hottest,

George Barker Smith, in that costume which obtained before the publication of the first fashions, was sitting at his desk in a conscientious endeavour to translate one paragraph of Cicero, which he held in his right hand, for every chapter of the Count of Monte Cristo, which he held in his left.

At his door suddenly appeared the Triumphant Egghead and Goat Phillips, whose title at this time had been conveyed solely for the butting manner of his attack. Each had likewise reached that stage of dishabille where there is little more to shed.

"Hello, old Sockbutts," said Egghead, genially.

"Hello yourself," returned Smith, non-committally.

"We're going up on the roof," continued the Egghead. "Anyone up yet?"

"Not yet."

"It's as hot as blazes," said the Goat. "Better come along."

"I ought to finish this Cicero," said Smith, wondering if he could leave his hero in a sack, ready to be plunged into the dizzy waters below.

"Oh, come on," said the Egghead; "I'll give you that when we come down. Have you any matches? I've got the coffin nails."

A slight shower had ended a few minutes before without bringing relief from the heat.

"Are you coming?" said the Egghead, already out of the window. "Don't be a grind, Smithy."

"Sure, I'm with you," replied Smith, thus forced to repel the insinuation.

The Goat had gone first, then the Egghead, with Smith bringing up the rear.

"Look out, fellows," whispered the pilot, lost in the darkness ahead. "It's slippery as the deuce!"

The way led up a gutter to the peak of one slope, down that, up another and over to a cranny which formed about the back chimneys. The still moist tiles were, in fact, slippery and treacherous, and their movements were made with calculation and solicitude.

Smith, arriving the last at the top of the first peak, waited until the Egghead had descended and climbed in safety to the next ridge, glanced down the twenty feet of slippery slate, and, tempted, called out:

"Look out, fellows, I'm going to slide!"

The Goat and the Egghead, in unison, cried to him to desist, for the second ridge which ended the slope of the first had a downward inclination towards the edge of the roof that made it exceedingly dangerous.

Just how it happened has never been satisfactorily settled: whether Smith actually intended to slide or whether he lost his grip and started unwillingly. However it may be, Egghead and the Goat, astride the second ridge, were suddenly horrified to see Smith's naked body shoot down the slope, strike the moist incline at the bottom, and, bounding down that, with increased velocity disappear over the roof. They heard one thud and then another in the gravel path, three stories below.

The two clung to each other with a dreadful sinking feeling.

"He's dead," said the Goat, solemnly. "Poor old Smith is dead."

"Squashed like a bug," said the Egghead. "We won't even recognise his remains."

"Egghead, it's all our fault—all our fault."

"Shut up, Goat, and don't blubber."

"I'm not."

"You are—for Heaven's sake, brace up! We've got to get down to him!"

They started fearfully over the treacherous return, reaching Smith's room thoroughly unnerved. Then they began to run down the stairs, calling out:

"Smithy's dead!"

"Smithy's fallen off the roof!"

On their trail came a motley assortment of excited boys, rushing out of every room. Without a single hope they tore around to the back of the Upper, and, there, sitting bolt upright in the position in which he had fallen, they found George Barker Smith. They stopped astounded.

"Smith, is that you!" Egghead said, in a hoarse, incredulous whisper, and the answer returned faintly:

"It's me, Egghead."

"Are you dying?"

"I don't know."

"Are your bones all broken?"

"I don't know—I'm full of gravel!"

The boys gazed astounded up at the dark outline three stories above them. Half-way, the slanting roof of the porch had broken the fall and saved him from certain death. They gazed in silence, and then the chorus arose:

"Holy cats!"

"Great snakes!"

" ' I don't know—I'm full of gravel!' "

" Marvellous ! "

" Can you beat that ! "

" Mamma ! "

" Simply marvellous ! "

Smith, still in a comatose condition, caught the sounds of astonishment, and suddenly comprehended, first, that he had done something without parallel in school history, and, second, that he was alive.

" You fellows, get me upstairs," he said, gruffly, " and send for Doctor Charlie. I want to get this gravel out of me."

Macnooder and Turkey reverently carried him to his room, while Shy Thomas, who was clothed in a dressing-gown, went streaming across the campus for the doctor.

A quick examination revealed the amazing fact that not a bone had been fractured.

" You've got a few bruises, and that's all, by George ! " said the doctor, looking at him in open-eyed wonder.

" It's the gravel that bothers me," said Smith, twisting on his side.

" You did sit down rather hard," remarked the doctor, with a twitch of his lips. In half an hour he had removed thirty-seven pieces of gravel, large and small, and departed, after ordering rest and a few days' sojourn in bed.

Hardly had the doctor departed when Hickey arrived, full of importance and enthusiasm. For a moment he stood at the foot of the bed surveying the bruised hero with the affectionate and fatherly joy of a Barnum suddenly discovering a new freak.

"My boy," he said, happily, "you're a wonder. You're great. You're it. There's been nothing like it ever happened. Smithy, my boy, you're a genius. You're the wonder of the age!"

"I suppose everyone's excited?" said Smith, faintly realising that Fate had touched him in her flight and made him famous.

"Excited? Why, they're howling with curiosity," responded Hickey, who, having cautiously turned the key in the door, returned and continued with importance:

"Say, but I suppose you don't realise what we can make of this, do you?"

"What do you mean?" said Smith.

"First, where are those thirty-seven pieces of gravel?"

"I threw them away."

"My boy, my boy!" said Hickey, sitting down

and burying his head in his arms. "Pearls before swine."

"But they're over there in the basket."

Hickey, with a cry of joy, flung himself on them, counted them and thrust them into his pocket.

"Smith," he said, condescendingly, "you've got certain qualities, I'll admit, but what you need is a manager!"

"Why, what are you thinking of?" said Smith, who began to have a suspicion of Hickey's plan.

"I suppose you would expose your honourable scars," said Hickey, disdainfully, "to any one who asks to see them?"

"Why not?"

"Just out of friendliness?"

"Yes."

"Smith, you *are* a nincompoop! Why, my boy, there's money in it—big money. Never thought of that, eh?"

"How so?"

"Exhibitions—paid exhibitions, my boy! We'll organise the greatest side-show ever known."

Smith blushed at the thought.

"Won't it be rather undignified?" he said doubtfully.

" Dignity, rats!" said Hickey. " Talk to me of dignity when you hear the gold rattling in your pocket, when you lodge in a marble palace and drive fast horses up Fifth Avenue. My boy, you don't known what you're worth. I'll have Macnooder paper the campus to-morrow. I'll get up scareheads that'll bring every mother's son of them scampering here to see you."

" What do I get out of it? " said Smith cautiously.

" Half! "

" You low-down robber! "

" Who had the idea? Would you ever have made a cent if it hadn't been for me? Do you suppose any attraction ever makes as much as his manager? My boy, I'm generous! I oughtn't to do it! Come now—is it a go? "

" Well—yes! "

" Wait—till you see the posters," said Hickey, squeezing his hand joyfully, " and mind, no private exhibitions. Promise? "

" I promise."

" Under oath? "

" So help me."

" Ta, ta."

Left at last alone, George Barker Smith could

hardly seize the full measure of his future. Hickey
was right, it was the biggest thing that had ever happened. In one short hour everything had changed.
Now he was of the elect—a part of history, a tale to
be told over whenever one old graduate would meet
another. Even Hungry Smeed's great pancake record would have to be placed second to this. Other
more distinguished appetites might come who would
achieve fifty pancakes, but no boy would ever go
the path he had gone. He was famous at last. At
Prom and Commencement he would be pointed out
to visitors in the company of Hickey, Flash Condit,
Cap Kiefer and Turkey Reiter. Only yesterday he
was plain George Barker Smith, to-morrow he might
be . . .

What would the morrow bring? Who would name
him? Would it be Hickey, Macnooder or Turkey or
the Egghead, or would some unsuspected classmate
find the happy expression? He hoped that it would be
something picturesque, but a little more dignified
than the Triumphant Egghead. He tried to imagine what the nickname would be. Of course, there
were certain obvious appellations that immediately
suggested themselves, such as Roofie, Jumper, or,
better still, Plunger Smith. There was also Tattoo

and Rubber and Sliding, but somehow none of these seemed to measure up to the achievement, and in this delightful perplexity Smith fell asleep.

OLD IRONSIDES
THE GREATEST SIDE-SHOW ON EARTH ON EXHIBITION
AT ROOM 67 UPPER
MANAGEMENT—Hicks & Macnooder.

Come one, Come all! Come and View the HUMAN METEOR, THE YOUNG RUBBER PLANT, THE FAMOUS PLUNGING ROCKET, THE WORLD-RENOWNED SMITH, THE BOY GRAVEL YARD!

Come and see the honourable scars! No private exhibition. This afternoon only! Old Ironsides is under contract not to bathe in the canal this fall. This is your one and only opportunity to see the results of Old Ironsides' encounter with the gravel path!

Come and see the 37 original guaranteed and authentic bits of gravel which dented but could not penetrate!

ADMISSION, 5 CENTS   FRESHMEN, 10 CENTS
$500 REWARD $500

To any one who will duplicate this mad, death-defying feat MR. MACNOODER, on behalf of Old Ironsides, will offer the above reward. Doctor's or Undertaker's bills to be shared in case of failure.

ROOM 67   ROOM 67
Exhibition begins at 2 o'clock.

The above posters, prominently displayed, produced a furore. By two o'clock fully one hundred boys were in line before room 67. At two o'clock Hickey addressed the crowd.

"Gentlemen, unfortunately a slight delay has become necessary—only a slight delay. Mr. Ironsides Smith's sense of natural delicacy is at present struggling with Mr. Ironsides Smith's desire not to disappoint his many friends and admirers. Just a slight delay, gentlemen—just a slight delay."

A cry of protest went up and Hickey disappeared. At the end of five minutes he returned radiant, announcing:

"Gentlemen, I am very glad to announce to you that Old Ironsides will not disappoint his many admirers. Only we wish it to be understood that this is a strictly scientific exhibition with an educational purpose in view. No levity will be tolerated. The exhibition is about to begin. Have your nickels in hand, gentlemen; ten cents for freshmen, with the privilege of shaking hands with Old Ironsides himself! Absolutely unique, absolutely unique!"

When the last spectator had filed out, Hickey, Macnooder and Smith divided fifteen dollars and twenty cents as pure profit, of which sum the gravel-stones had brought no less than a third.

When on the fourth day Smith was able painfully

to descend the stairs and circulate in the world again he felt the full delight of his newly-acquired fame. At the jigger-shop, Al graciously waved aside his tendered money, saying:

"I guess it's up to me, Ironsides, to stand treat. Such things don't happen every day. Go ahead—do your worst."

Bill Appleby and " Mista " Laloo, the rival livery men, Bill Orum, the cobbler, Barnum of the village store, even Doc Cubberly, the bell-ringer, with his little dog, stopped to watch him pass. When he crossed the campus youngsters gambolled up to his side with solicitous inquiries and the inevitable:

" Say, weren't you awfully scared? "

Even in the classroom the Roman, after flunking him, would say:

" That will do now, Smith. You may sit down— gently."

So he was now " Old Ironsides." He liked the name and was proud of it. It had a certain grim, uncompromising sternness about it that lent it dignity. It sounded well and it had patriotic associations.

For a whole week he knew the intoxication of popularity, of being the celebrity of the hour, of the thrill that runs up and down the back when a dozen glances are following, and the music of a murmured name, admiringly pronounced. Then abruptly another hero was exalted and he fell.

One evening after supper, while the fourth form lounged on the esplanade of the Upper, Turkey Reiter and Slugger Jones amused themselves with teasing Goat Phillips, who, being privileged by his diminutive size, responded by butting his tormentors in vigorous fashion.

"My, what an awful rambunctious, great big Goat," said Reiter, defending himself. "Do goats eat neckties?"

"I'll eat yours," responded the youngster recklessly.

"Ten double jiggers to one you can't do it," said Slugger Jones, lazily.

"Give me the tie," responded Phillips.

More to continue the joke than for any other reason, Turkey detached the green and yellow cross tie, which was his joy, and tendered it. What was his amazement to see Goat Phillips calmly set to work to devour it, and to devour it to the very last shred in the most classic goat-fashion.

When he had swallowed the last mouthful he stood stock-still and gazed at his shrieking audience. Then he began to have doubts; then he began to have premonitions. Then he ended by having settled on rather the most unsettling convictions. The consideration of the act came after the accomplishment, but it came with terrifying force. What would happen now?

"Turkey," he said, grown very solemn, "you don't think I'm going to be poisoned, do you?"

Turkey became serious at once. Everyone became serious.

"What do you fellows think?" said Turkey, addressing the crowd.

No one had any opinions to volunteer. There were no precedents to go by.

"He might get ptomaine poisoning," finally suggested Shy Thomas.

"What's that?" said Goat, horrified. Shy was forced to confess that he did not know. Hungry Smeed thought it was when you cut your toe on an oyster shell.

"See here, Goat," said Turkey, decisively, "we can't fool with this any more. You come with me."

The now thoroughly demoralised and penitent Goat went meekly between Turkey and Slugger toward Foundation House. But on the way, encountering the Roman, they decided to consult him instead.

"Please, sir," said Phillips, with difficult calm, "I'd like to ask you something."

The master stopped and, prepared for any eventuality, said:

"Well, Phillips, nothing serious, I hope?"

"Please, sir, I'm afraid it is," said Phillips, all in a breath. "I've just eaten a necktie, sir."

"A what?"

"A necktie, sir, and I want to know if you think I'm in any danger, sir."

The Roman stood stock-still for a long moment, with dropped jaw; then, recovering himself, he said:

"A necktie, Phillips?"

"Yes, sir."

"A whole necktie?"

"Yes, sir."

"Well, Phillips, if you can eat a necktie I guess you can digest it!"

*   *   *   *   *

The next morning, when Ironsides Smith unsuspectingly strolled out into the campus, no soul did him honour, not a glance turned as he turned, not a first form youngster, primed with curiosity and admiration, came rushing to his side. Instead, a knot of boys at the far end of the esplanade were clustered in excited contemplation about Goat Phillips, the boy who had heroically eaten a necktie rather than suffer a dare.

Then Ironsides understood—he was the hero of yesterday. A new celebrity had risen for the delectation of the fickle populace. The King was dead —long live the King!

He went to the classroom disillusionised and sat through the hour stolidly tasting the bitterness of Napoleonic isolation. So this was the favour of crowds. In a night to be dethroned and forgotten!

As he descended Memorial steps, Goat Phillips passed, radiant, saluted by capricornian acclamations.

Smith regarded him darkly.

"As though any one couldn't eat a necktie," he said in righteous disgust.

Unacclaimed he went through the crowd toward the Upper—he who had risked life and limb to amuse them for a week!

From a tower window in the Upper the Triumphant Egghead, lolling on the cushioned window-seat, called down lazily:

"Oh, you—Ironsides!"

That was the answer. [Let popularity run after a dozen unworthy lights. Other boys would come who would eat neckties, no one ever would go the way he had gone. He had nothing to do with transitory emotions. He must be superior to the voice of the hour. He, Ironsides, belonged to history. That, nothing could take from him!

THE PROTEST AGAINST SINKERS

THE feeling of revolt sprang up at chapel during the head master's weekly talk. Ordinarily the school awaited these moments with expectation, received them with tolerance and drew from them all the humour that could be extracted.

These little heart-to-heart talks brought joy to many an overweighted brain and obliterated momentarily the slow, dragging months of slush and hail.

194

They also added, from time to time, picturesque expressions to the school vocabulary—and for that much was forgiven them. No one who heard it will ever forget the slashing that descended from the rostrum on the demon tobacco, in its embodied vice, the cigarette, nor the chill that ran over each of the four hundred cigarette smokers as the head master, with his boring glance straight on him, concluded:

"Yes, I know what you boys will say; I know what your plea will be when you are caught. You will come to me and you'll say with tears in your eyes, with tears:

"'Doctor, think of my mother—my poor mother —it will kill my mother!'

"I tell you, *now* is the time to think of your mother; *now* is the time to spare her grey hairs. Every cigarette you boys smoke is a *nail in the coffin of your mother.*"

It was terrific. The school was unanimous in its verdict that the old man had outdone himself. Boys, whom a whiff of tobacco rendered instantly ill, smoked up the ventilators that night with shivers of delight, and from that day to this a cigarette has never been called anything but a coffin-nail.

Only the week before, in announcing the suspension of Corkscrew Higgins (since with the ministry), for, among other offences, mistaking the initials on the hat of Bucky Oliver as his own, the head master in his determination to abolish forever such deadly practices, had given forth the following:

" Young gentlemen, it is my painful duty, my very painful duty, to announce to you the suspension of the boy Higgins. The boy Higgins was a sloth, the boy Higgins was the prince of sloths! The boy Higgins was a gambler, the boy Higgins was the prince of gamblers! The boy Higgins was a liar, the boy Higgins was the prince of liars! The boy Higgins was a thief, the boy Higgins was the prince of thieves! Therefore, the boy Higgins will no longer be a member of this community!"

The school pardoned the exaggeration in its admiration for the rhetoric, which was rated up to the oration against Catiline. But on the first Monday of that lean month of February the school rose in revolt. In a tirade against the alarming decline in the percentage of scholastic marks the head master, flinging all caution to the winds, had terminated with these incendiary words:

" I know what the trouble is, and I'll tell you. The trouble with you boys is INORDINATE and IM-

MODERATE EATING. The trouble with you boys is
—You Eat Too Much!"

Such a groan as went up! To comprehend the
monstrosity of the accusation it is not sufficient to
have been a boy; one must have retained the memory
of the sharp pains and gnawing appetites of those
growing days! Four hundred-odd famished forms,
just from breakfast, suddenly galvanised by that
unmerited blow, roared forth a unanimous indignant:

" *What!* "

" Eat too much!"—they could hardly believe their
ears. Had the head master of the school, with years
of personal experience, actually, in his sober mind,
proclaimed that they ate too much! The words had
been said; the accusation had to stand. And such
a time to proclaim it—in the month of sliced bananas
and canned vegetables! The protest that rumbled
and growled in the under-form houses exploded in
the Dickinson.

It so happened that for days there had been a
dull grumbling about the monotony of the daily
meals and the regularity and frequency of the appearance of certain abhorrent dishes, known as
" scrag-birds and sinkers." " Scrag-bird " was a
generic term, allowing a wide latitude for conjecture,

but " sinker " was an opprobrious epithet dedicated
to a particularly hard, doughy substance that under more favourable auspices sometimes, without fear
of contradiction, achieves the name of " dumpling."

The " sinker " was, undoubtedly, the deadliest enemy of the growing boy—the most persistent, the
most malignant. It knew no laws and it defied all
restraint. It languished in the spring, but thrived
and multiplied amazingly in the canned, winter term.
It was as likely to bob up in a swimming dish of
boiled chicken as it was certain to accompany a
mutton stew. It associated at times with veal and
attached itself to corned beef; it concealed itself in
a beefsteak pie and clung to a leg of lamb. What
the red rag is to the bull, the pudgy white of the
" sinker " was to the boys, who, in a sort of desperate
hope of exterminating the species, never allowed one
to return intact to the kitchen. Twice a week was
the allotted appearance of the " sinker "; at a third
visit grumbling would break out; at a fourth arose
threats of leaving for Andover or Exeter, of writing
home, of boycotting the luncheon.

Now, it so happened that during the preceding
week the " sinker " had inflicted itself not four, but
actually six, times on that community of aching

voids. The brutal accusation of the head master was the spark to the powder. The revolt assumed head and form during the day, and a call for a meeting of protest was unanimously made for that very night.

The boys met with the spirit of the Boston Tea Party, resolved to defend their liberties and assert their independence. The inevitable Doc Macnooder was to address the meeting. He spoke naturally, fluently, with great sounding phrases, on any occasion, on any topic, for his own pure delight, and he always continued to speak until violently suppressed.

"Fellows," he began, without apologies to history —"we are met to decide once and for all whether we are a free governing body, to ask ourselves what is all this worth? For weeks we have endured, supinely on our backs, the tyranny of Mrs. Van Asterbilt, the matron of this House. We have, I say, supinely permitted each insult to pass unchallenged. But the hour has struck, the worm has turned, the moment has come and, without the slightest hesitation, I ask you . . . I ask you . . . what do I ask you?" he paused, and appealed for enlightenment.

The meeting found him guilty of levity and threatened him with the ban of silence.

Macnooder looked grieved and continued: " I ask you to strike as your fathers struck. I ask you to string the bow, to whet the knife, to sharpen the tomahawk, to loose the dogs of war——"

Amid a storm of whoops and catcalls, Macnooder was pulled back into his seat. He rose and explained that his peroration was completed and demanded the inalienable right to express his opinions.

The demand was rejected by a vote of eighty-two to one (Macnooder voting).

Butcher Stevens rose with difficulty and, clutching the shoulder of Red Dog in front of him, addressed the gathering as follows:

" Fellows, I am no silver-tongued orator and all I want to say is just a few words. I think we want to treat this thing seriously." (Cries of " Hear! hear!" " Right.") " I think, fellows, this is a very serious matter, and I think we ought to take some action. This food matter is getting pretty bad. I don't think, fellows, that we ought to stand for ' sinkers ' the way they're coming at us, without some action. I don't know just what action we ought to take, but I think we ought really to take some action."

The Butcher subsided into his seat amid immense applause. Lovely Mead arose and jangling the keys in his trousers pocket, addressed the ceiling in rapid, jerky periods:

"Fellows, I think we ought to begin by taking a vote—a vote. I think—I think the sentiment of this meeting is about made up—made up. I think my predecessor has very clearly expressed the—the— has voiced the sentiments of this meeting—very clearly. I think a vote would clear the air, therefore I move we take a vote."

He sighed contentedly and returned into the throng. Doc Macnooder sarcastically demanded what they were to vote upon. Lovely Mead, in great confusion, rose and stammered:

"I meant to say, Mr. Chairman, that I move we take a vote, take a vote to—to take some action."

"Action about what?" said the merciless Macnooder.

Lovely Mead remained speechless. Hungry Smeed interposed glibly:

"Mister Chairman, I move that it is the sense of this meeting that we should take some action looking toward the remedying of the present condition of our daily meals."

The motion was passed and the chairman announced that he was ready to hear suggestions as to the nature of the act, as contemplated. A painful silence succeeded.

Macnooder rose and asked permission to offer a suggestion. The demand was repulsed. Wash Simmons moved that at the next appearance of the abhorrent "sinkers," they should rise and leave the room *en masse*. It was decided that the plan entailed too many sacrifices, and it was rejected.

Crazy Opdyke from the Woodhull developed the following scheme, full of novelty and imagination:

"I say, fellows, I've got an idea, you know. What we want is an object lesson, you know, something striking. Now, fellows, this is what I propose: We're eighty-five of us in these dining-rooms; now, at two 'sinkers' each, that makes one hundred and seventy 'sinkers' every time; at six times that makes one thousand 'sinkers' a week. What we want to do is to carry off the 'sinkers' from table, save them up, and at the end of the week make a circle of them around the campus as an object lesson!"

Macnooder, again, was refused permission to speak

in support of this measure, which had an instant appeal to the imagination of the audience. In the end, however, the judgment of the more serious prevailed, and the motion was lost by a close vote. After more discussion the meeting finally decided to appoint an embassy of three, who should instantly proceed to the head master's, and firmly lay before him the Woodhull's and the Dickinson's demand for unconditional and immediate suppression of that indigestible and totally ornamental article known as " the sinker." Hickey, Wash Simmons and Crazy Opdyke, by virtue of their expressed defiance, were chosen to carry the ultimatum. Some one proposed that Macnooder should go as a fourth, and the motion passed without opposition. Macnooder rose and declined the honour, but asked leave to state his reasons. Whereupon the meeting adjourned.

The Messrs. Crazy Opdyke, Hickey, and Wash Simmons held a conference and decided to shave and assume creased trousers in order to render the aspect of their mission properly impressive. After a short delay they united on the steps, where they received the exhortations of their comrades—to speak out boldly, to mince no words, and to insist on their demands.

The distance to Foundation House, where the head master resided, was short—thirty seconds in the darkness; and almost before they knew it the three were at the door. There, under the muffled lamp, they stopped, with spontaneous accord, and looked at one another.

"I say," said Hickey, "hadn't we better agree on what we'll say to the old man? We want to be firm, you know."

"That's a good idea," Opdyke assented, and Wash added, "We'll take a turn down the road."

"Now, what's your idea?" said Simmons to Hickey, when they had put a safe distance between them and the residence of the Doctor.

"We'd better keep away from discussion," replied Hickey. "The Doctor'll beat us out there, and I don't think we'd better be too radical either, because we want to be firm."

"What do you call radical?" said Opdyke, with a little defiance.

"Well, now, we don't want to be too aggressive; we don't want to go in with a chip on our shoulder."

"Hickey, you're beginning to hedge!"

Hickey indignantly denied the accusation, and a

little quarrel arose between them, terminated by Wash, who broke in:

"Shut up, Crazy—Hickey is dead right. We want to go in friendly-like, just as though we knew the Doctor would side with us at once—sort of take him into our confidence."

"That's it," said Hickey; "we want to be good-natured at first, lay the matter before him calmly, then afterward we can be firm.

"Rats!" said Crazy; "are we going to tell him, or not, that we represent the Dickinson and the Woodhull and that they have voted the extinction of 'sinkers'?"

"Sure we are!" exclaimed Wash. "You don't think we are afraid, do you?"

"Well, then, let's tell him," said Crazy. "Come on, if you're going to."

They returned resolutely and again entered the dominion of the dreary lamp.

"Say, fellows," Wash suddenly interjected, "are we going to say anything about 'scrag-birds'?"

"Sure," said Crazy.

"The deuce we are!" said Hickey.

"Why not?" said Crazy, militantly.

" Because we don't want to make fools of ourselves."

The three withdrew again and threshed out the point. It was decided to concentrate on the " sinker." Crazy gave in because he said he was cold.

" Well, now, it's all settled," said Hickey. " We make a direct demand for knocking out the ' sinker,' and we stand firm on that. Nothing else. Come on."

" Come on."

A third time they came to the terrible door.

" I say," said Wash, suddenly, " we forgot. Who's to do the talking? "

" Crazy, of course," said Hickey, looking hard at Simmons, " since that clapper episode, I'm not dropping in for the dessert! "

" Sure, Crazy, you're just the one," Simmons agreed.

" Hold up," said Crazy, whose fury suddenly cooled. " Let's talk that over."

Again they retired for deliberation.

" Now, see here, fellows," said Crazy, " let's be reasonable. We want this thing to go through, don't we? "

" Who's hedging now? " said Hickey, with a laugh.

" No one," retorted Crazy. " I'll talk up if you

say. I'm not afraid, only I don't stand one, two, three with the Doctor and you know it. I've flunked every recitation in Bible this month. What we want is the strongest pull—and Wash is the one. Why, the old man would feed out of Wash's hand."

Wash indignantly repelled the insinuation. Finally it was agreed that Crazy should state the facts, that Hickey should say, " Doctor, we feel strongly, very strongly, about this," and that Wash should then make the direct demand for the suspension for one month of the " sinker," and its future regulation to two appearances a week.

" And now, no more backing and filling," said Hickey.

" I'll lay the facts before him, all right," added Crazy, clenching his fists.

" We'll stick together, and we stand firm," said Wash. " Now for it! "

They had reached a point about thirty feet from the threshold, when suddenly the door was flung violently open and a luckless boy bolted out, under the lamp, so that the three could distinguish the vehement gestures. The Doctor appeared in a passion of rage, calling after the retreating offender:

" Don't you dare, young man, to come to me again

with such a complaint. You get your work up to where it ought to be, or down you go, and there isn't a power in this country that can prevent it."

The door slammed violently and silence returned.

" He's not in a very receptive mood," said Wash, after a long pause.

" Not precisely," said Hickey, thoughtfully.

" I'm catching cold," said Crazy.

" Suppose we put it over?" continued Wash. "What do you say, Hickey?"

" I shall not oppose the will of the majority."

" And you, Crazy?"

" I think so, too."

They returned to the Dickinson, where they were surrounded and assailed with questions: How had the Doctor taken it?—What had he said?

" We took no talk from him," said Crazy, with a determined shake of his head, and then Wash added brusquely, " Just keep your eyes on the ' sinkers.' "

" You took long enough," put in the suspicious Macnooder.

" We were firm," replied Hickey, bristling at the recollection—" very firm!"

BEAUTY'S SISTER

His hair it is a faded white,
    His eye a watery blue;
He has no buttons on his coat,
    No shoe-strings in his shoe.

" BEAUTY " SAWTELLE, or Chesterton V. Sawtelle,
as it was pronounced when each Monday the master
of the form read the bi-weekly absences from bath,
sat adjusting his skate on the edge of the pond, with
a look of ponderous responsibility on the freckled
face, crowned by a sheaf of tow hair, like the wisp

of a Japanese doll. Presently he drew from his pocket a dance-card, glanced over it for the twentieth time, and replaced it with a sigh.

"Cracky!" he said, in despair. "Sixteen regulars and eight extras; sixteen and eight, twenty-four. Gee!"

Beauty's heart was heavy, and his hope faint, for the sinister finger of the Prom had cast its shadow over the lighthearted democracy of boyhood. Into this free republic, where no thoughts of the outside society should penetrate, the demoralising swish of coming petticoats had suddenly intruded its ominous significance of a world without, where such tyrannies as money and birth stand ready to divide the unsuspecting hosts.

Now Beauty's woes were manifold: he was only a second former, and the Prom was the property of the lords of the school, the majestic fourth formers, who lived in the Upper House, and governed themselves according to the catalogue and a benevolent tempering of the exact theory of independence.

A few rash under-formers with pretty sisters were admitted on sufferance, and robbed of their partners if the chance arose. Beauty, scrubby boy of fourteen, with a like aversion to girls and stiff col-

lars in his ugly little body, had been horrified to
learn that his sister, at the invitation of Rogers,
the housemaster, was coming to the Prom. On his
shoulders devolved the herculean task of filling a
card from the upper class, only a handful of whom
he knew, at a moment when the cards had been cir-
culated for weeks. So he stood dejectedly, calculating how to fill the twenty-four spaces that were
so blank and interminable. Twenty-four dances to
fill, and the Prom only two weeks off!

In the middle of the pond boys were darting and
swaying in a furious game of hockey. Beauty lingered, biding his opportunity, searching the crowd
for a familiar face, until presently Wash Simmons,
emerging from the mêlée, darted to his side, grind-
ing his skates and coming to a halt for breath, with
a swift: "Hello, Venus! How's the Dickinson these
days?"

Beauty, murmuring an inaudible reply, stood
turning and twisting, desperately seeking to frame a
demand.

"What's the secret sorrow, Beauty?" continued
Wash, with a glance of surprise.

"I say, Wash," said Beauty, plunging—"I say,
have you got any dances left?"

" I? Oh, Lord, no!" said the pitcher of the school nine, with a quick glance. "Gone long ago."

He drew the strap tight, dug his hands into his gloves again, and with a nod flashed back into the crowd. Beauty, gulping down something that rose in his throat, started aimlessly to skirt the edge of the pond. He had understood the look that Wash had given him in that swift moment.

In this abstracted mood, he suddenly came against something angular and small that accompanied him to the ice with a resounding whack.

"Clumsy beast!" said a sharp voice.

From his embarrassed position, Beauty recognised the Red Dog.

"Excuse me, Red Dog," he said hastily; "I didn't see you."

"Why, it's Beauty," said the Red Dog, rubbing himself. "Blast you! all the same."

"I say, Red Dog," said Beauty, "have you any dances left?"

" All gone, Beauty," answered Red Dog, stooping suddenly to recover his skate.

"Nothing left?"

"Nope—filled the last extra to-day," said Red Dog, with the shining face of prevarication. Then he added, "Why, Venus, are *you* going to the Prom?"

"No," said Sawtelle; "it's my sister."

"Oh, I'm sorry. I'd like to oblige you, but you see how it is," said Red Dog, lamely.

"I see."

"Ta, ta, Beauty! So long!"

Sawtelle shut his lips, struck a valiant blow at an imaginary puck, and began to whistle.

> 'Tis a jolly life we lead
> Care and sorrow we defy—

After piping forth this inspiring chorus with vigorous notes, the will gave way. He began another:

> To Lawrenceville my father sent me,
> Where for college I should prepare;
>   And so I settled down,
>   In this queer, forsaken town,
> About five miles away from anywhere.

The bellows gave out. Overcome by the mournfulness of the last verse, he dropped wearily on the bank, continuing doggedly:

About five miles from anywhere, my boys,
Where old Lawrenceville evermore shall stand;
For has she not stood,
Since the time of the flood—

Whether the accuracy of the last statement or the forced rhyme displeased him, he broke off, heaved a sigh, and said viciously: " They lied, both of 'em."

" Well, how's the boy? " said a familiar voice.

Beauty came out of the vale of bitterness to perceive at his side the great form of Turkey Reiter, preparing to adjust his skates.

" Oh, Turkey," said Beauty, clutching at the straw, " I've been looking everywhere——"

" What's the matter? "

" Turkey, I'm in an awful hole."

" Out with it."

" I say, Turkey," said Sawtelle, stumbling and blushing—" I say, you know, my sister's coming to the Prom, and I thought if you'd like—that is, I wanted to know if—if you wouldn't take her dance-card and get it filled for me." Then he added abjectly: " I'm awfully sorry."

Turkey looked thoughtful. This was a commission he did not relish. Beauty looked particularly unattractive that afternoon, in a red tobogganing toque that swore at his faded white hair, and the orange freckles that stared out from every point of vantage.

" Why, Beauty," he began hesitatingly, " the way it is, you see, my card's already filled, and I'm afraid, honestly, that's about the case with all the others."

" She's an awfully nice girl," said Sawtelle, looking down in a desperate endeavour to control his voice.

" Nice girl," thought Turkey, " ahem! Yes; must be a good-looker, too, something on Venus's particular line of beauty."

He glanced at his companion, and mentally pictured a lanky girl, with sandy hair, a little upstart nose, and a mass of orange freckles. But between Turkey and Sawtelle relations had been peculiar. There had been many moments in the last year at the Dickinson when the ordinary luxuries of life would have been difficult had it not been for the superior financial standing of Chesterton V. Sawtelle. The account had been a long one, and there was a slight haziness in Turkey's mind as to the exact status of the balance. Also, Turkey was genuinely grateful, with that sense of gratitude which is described as a lively looking forward to favours to come.

"Oh, well, young un," he said with rough good humour, "give us the card. I'll do what I can. But, mind you, I can't take any myself. My card's full, and it wouldn't do for me to cut dances."

Jumping up, he started to escape the effusive thanks of the overjoyed Sawtelle, but suddenly wheeled and came skating back.

"Hello, Beauty!" he called out, "I say, what's your sister's name?"

"Sally—that is, Sarah," came the timid answer.

"Heavens!" said Turkey to himself as he flashed over the ice. "That settles it. Sally—Sally! A nice pickle I'm in! Wonder if she sports spectacles and old-fashioned frocks. A nice pickle—I'll be the laughing stock of the whole school. Guess I won't have much trouble recognising Beauty's sister. Whew! That comes from having a kind heart!"

With these and similar pleasant reflections he threaded his way among the crowd of skaters until at length he perceived Hickey skimming over the ice, stealing the puck from a bunch of scrambling players, until his progress checked, and the puck vanishing into a distant mêlée, he came to a stop for breath. Turkey, profiting by the occasion, descended on his victim.

"Whoa there, Hickey!"

"Whoa it is!"

"How's your dance-card?"

"A dazzling galaxy of beauty, a symposium of grace, a feast of——"

"Got anything left? I have a wonder for you if you have."

"Sure; twelfth regular and sixth extra—but the duchess will be awfully cut up."

"Twelfth and sixth," said Turkey, with a nod; "that's a go."

"Who's the heart-smasher?" asked Hickey, with an eye on the approaching puck.

"A wonder, Hickey; a screamer. There'll be nothing to it. Ta, ta! Much obliged."

"What's her name?"

"Sawtelle—some distant relative of the Beauty's, I believe. I'm filling out her card. Obliged for the dance. Ta, ta!"

"Hold up!" said Hickey, quickly. "Hold up! Jiminy! I almost forgot—why, I do believe I went and promised those two to Hasbrouck. Isn't that a shame! Sorry. To think of my forgetting that! Try to give you some other. Confound it! I have no luck." -With the most mournful look in the world

he waved his hand and sped ostentatiously toward
the bunch of players.

"Hickey's on to me," thought Turkey as he
watched him disengage himself from the crowd and
skate off with Sawtelle; "no hope in that quarter."

Finally, after an hour's persistent work, during
which he pleaded and argued, commanded and threatened, he succeeded in filling exactly six of the necessary twenty-four dances. Indeed, he would have had
no difficulty in completing the card if he could have
passed over that fatal name. But each time, just as
he was congratulating himself on another conquest,
his victim would ask, "By the way, what name shall
I put down?"

"Oh—er—Miss Sawtelle," he would answer nonchalantly; "a distant relative of the Beauty—
though nothing like him—ha! ha!"

Then each would suddenly remember that the
dances in question were already half-promised,—a
sort of an understanding; but of course he would
have to look it up,—but of course, if he found they
were free, why, then of course, he wanted, above all
things in the world, to dance with Miss Sawtelle.

"Well, anyhow," said Turkey to himself, recapitu-

lating, " I've got six, provided they don't all back
out. Let me see. I can make the Kid take three,—
that's nine,—and Snookers will have to take three,—
that's twelve,—and, hang it! Butcher and Egghead have got to take two each—that would make
sixteen. The other eight I can fill up with some
harmless freaks: some will snap at anything."

That night at the supper-table Turkey had to
face the music.

" You're a nice one, you are," said Hickey,
starting in immediately, " you arch deceiver. You
are a fine friend; I have my opinion of you. 'Handsome girl,' ' a wonder,' ' fine talker,' ' a screamer '—
that's the sort of game you try on your friends, is
it? Who is she? Oh—ah, yes, a *distant* relative of
the Beauty."

" What's up now? " said the Kid, editor of the
" Lawrence," and partner of Turkey's secrets, joys,
and debts.

" Hasn't he tried to deceive you yet? " continued
Hickey, with an accusing look at Turkey. " No?
That's a wonder! What do you think of a fellow
who tries to pass off on his friends such a girl as the
Beauty's sister? "

"No!" said Butcher Stevens.

"What!" exclaimed Macnooder, laying down his knife with a thud.

"Beauty's sister," said the Egghead, gaping with astonishment.

"Well, why not?" said Turkey, defiantly.

"Listen to that!" continued Hickey. "The brazenness of it!"

The four graduates of the Dickinson, after a moment of stupefied examination of Hickey and Reiter, suddenly burst into roars of laughter that produced a craning of necks and a storm of inquiries from the adjoining tables.

When the hilarity had been somewhat checked, Hickey returned to the persecution of the blushing Turkey.

"Bet you three to one she's a mass of freckles," he said. "Bet you even she wears glasses; bet you one to three she's cross-eyed; bet you four to one she won't open her mouth."

"Hang you, Hickey!" said Turkey, flushing, "I won't have her talked about so."

"Did you take any dances?" said the Kid to Hickey.

"Me?" exclaimed the latter, in great dudgeon.

"Me! Well, I guess not! I wouldn't touch any of that tribe with a ten-foot pole."

"Look here, you fellows have got to shut up," said Turkey, forced at last into a virtuous attitude by the exigency of the situation. "I promised the Beauty I'd fill his sister's card for him, and I'm going to do it. The girl can't help her looks. You talk like a lot of cads. What you fellows ought to do is to join in and give her a treat. The girl is probably from the backwoods, and this ought to be made the time of her life."

"Turkey," said the malicious Hickey, "how many dances have you eagerly appropriated?"

Turkey stopped point-blank, greeted by derisive jeers.

"Oho!"

"That's it, is it?"

"Fake!"

"Humbug!"

"Not at all," said Turkey, indignantly. "What do you think I am?"

"Pass over your list and let's see the company you're going to introduce her to," said Hickey, stretching out his hand for the dance-card. "Ah, I must congratulate you, my boy; your selection

is magnificent; the young lady will be charmed."
He flipped the card disdainfully to the Egghead,
saying, "A bunch of freaks!"

"Hang it all!" said the Egghead, "that's too
hard on any girl. A fine opinion she'll have of Lawrenceville fellows! We can't stand for that."

"Look here," said the Kid, suddenly. "Turkey
is at fault, and has got to be punished. Here's what
we'll do, though: let's each take a dance on condition
that Turkey takes her out to supper."

"Oh, I say!" protested Turkey, who had other
plans.

The others acclaimed the plan gleefully, rejoicing
in his discomfiture, until Turkey, driven to a corner,
was forced to capitulate.

That evening on the esplanade he called Snookers
to him, and resting his hand affectionately on the
little fellow's shoulder, said: "Old man, do you
want to do me a favour?"

"Sure."

"I'm filling up a girl's card for the Prom, and
I want you to help me out."

"Certainly; give me a couple, if the girl's the real
thing."

"Much obliged. I'll put your name down."

"Second and fifth. Say, who is she?"

"Oh, some relative of Sawtelle's—you remember you used to go with him a good deal in the Dickinson. It's his sister."

"Whew!" said Snookers, with a long-drawn whistle. "Say, give me three more, will you?"

"Hardly," answered Turkey, with a laugh; "but I'll spare you another."

"I didn't think it quite fair to the girl," he explained later, "to give her too big a dose of Snookers. Queer, though, how eager the little brute was!"

The last week dragged interminably in multiplied preparations for the great event. In the evenings the war of strings resounded across the campus from the "gym," where the Banjo and Mandolin clubs strove desperately to perfect themselves for the concert. The Dramatic Club, in sudden fear, crowded the day with rehearsals, while from the window of Room 65, Upper, the voice of Biddy Hampton, soloist of the Glee Club, was heard chanting "The Pride of the House is Papa's Baby" behind doors stout enough to resist the assaults of his neighbours.

Oil-stoves and flatirons immediately came into demand, cushions were rolled back from window-seats, and trousers that were limp and discouraged, grew smooth and well-creased under the pressure of the hot iron.   Turkey and Doc Macnooder, who from their long experience in the Dickinson had become expert tailors, advertised on the bulletin board:

REITER AND MACNOODER.
Bon Ton Tailors

Trousers neatly pressed, at fifteen cents per pair; all payments strictly cash—*in advance.*

Each night the dining-room of the Upper was cleared, and the extraordinary spectacle was seen of boys of all sizes in sweaters and jerseys, clasping each other desperately around the waist, spinning and bumping their way about the reeling room to the chorus of:

"Get off my feet!"

"Reverse, you lubber!"

"Now, *one*, two, three——"

"A fine lady you are!"

"Do you expect me to carry you around the room?"

"Darn you, fatty!"

"Trousers that were limp and discouraged,
grew smooth"

" Hold tight! "

" Let 'er rip now! "

From the end of the room the cynics and misog-ynists, roosting on the piled-up tables and chairs, croaked forth their contempt:

" Oh, you fussers! "

" You lady-killers! "

" Dance, my darling, dance! "

" Squeeze her tight, Bill! "

" That's the way! "

" Look at Skinny! "

" Keep a-hoppin', Skinny! "

" Look at him spin! "

" For heaven's sake, someone stop Skinny! "

Of evenings certain of the boys would wander in pairs to the edge of the woods and confide to each other the secret attachments and dark, forlorn hopes that were wasting them away. Turkey and the Kid, who were going as stags, opened their hearts to each other and spoke of the girl, the one distant girl, whose image not all the fair faces that would come could for a moment dim.

" Kid," said Turkey, in solemn conclusion, speak-ing from the experience of eighteen years, " I am going to make that little girl—my wife."

"Turkey, old man, God bless you!" answered the confidant, with nice regard for old precedents. Then he added, a little choked, "Turkey, I, too—I——"

"I understand, Kid," said Turkey, gravely clapping his shoulder; "I've known it all along."

"Dear old boy!"

They walked in silence.

"What's her name?" asked Turkey, slowly.

"Lucille. And hers?"

"Marie Louise."

Another silence.

"Kid, is it all right?"

The romanticist considered a moment, and then shook his head.

"No, Turk."

"Dear old boy, you'll win out."

"I must. And you, Turk, does she care?"

A heavy sigh was the answer. They walked back arm in arm, each fully believing in the other's sorrow, and almost convinced of his own. At the esplanade of the Upper they stopped and listened to the thumping of the piano and the systematic beat from the dancers.

"I wish it were all over," said Turkey, gloomily. "This can mean nothing to me."

"Nor to me," said the Kid, staring at the melancholy moon.

On the fateful day the school arose, so to speak, as one boy, shaved, and put on a clean collar. Every boot was blacked, every pair of trousers creased to a cutting edge. The array of neckties that suddenly appeared in gigantic puffs or fluttering wings was like the turn of autumn in a single night.

Chapel and the first two recitations over, the esplanade of the Upper was crowded with fourth formers, circulating critically in the dandified throng, chattering excitedly of the coming event. Perish the memory of the fashion there displayed! It seemed magnificent then: let that be the epitaph.

The bell called, and the group slowly departed to the last recitation. From each house a stream of boys came pouring out and made their lagging way around the campus toward Memorial. Slower and slower rang the bell, and faster came the unwilling slaves—those in front with dignity; those behind with despatch, and so on down the line to the last scattered stragglers, who came racing over the lawns. The last peal sounded, the last laggard tore up Memorial steps, and vanished within. A moment later the gong in the hall clanged, and the next recitation was on. The circle, a moment before alive with figures, was quiet and deserted. A group of seven or eight lounging on the esplanade were chatting indolently, tossing a ball back and forth with the occupant of a third-story window.

At this moment Turkey emerged from the doorway in shining russets, a Gladstone collar, a tie of robin's-egg-blue, and a suit of red and green plaids, such as the innocent curiosity of a boy on his first allow-ance goes to with the thirst of possession.

"Hurrah for Turkey!" cried the Kid. "He looks like a regular fashion-plate."

In an instant he was surrounded, punched, ex-amined, and complimented.

"Well, fellows, it's time to give ourselves them finishing touches," said the Egghead, with a glance of envy. "Turkey is trying to steal a march on us. The girls are coming."

"Hello!" cried the Kid, suddenly. "Who's this?"

All turned. From behind Foundation House came a carriage. It drove on briskly until nearly opposite the group on the steps, when the driver reined in, and some one within looked out dubi-ously.

"'Get off my feet!. . A fine lady you are!'"

"Turkey, you're in luck," said the Gutter Pup. "You're the only one with the rouge on. Go down gracefully and see what the lady wants."

So down went Turkey to his duty. They watched him approach the carriage and speak to some one inside. Then he closed the door and spoke to the driver, evidently pointing out his destination, for the cab continued around the circle.

Then Turkey made a jump for the esplanade, and, deaf to all inquiries, seized upon his roommate and dragged him aside.

"Great guns! Kid," he exclaimed, "I've seen her—Beauty's sister! She isn't like Beauty at all. She's a stunner, a dream! Look here! Get that dance-card. Get it, if you have to lie and steal. He's in recitation now. You've got to catch him when he comes out. For heaven's sake! don't let anyone get ahead of you. Tell him two girls have backed out, and I want five more dances. Tell him I'm to take her to the debate to-night, and the Dramatic Club to-morrow. Kid, get that card!"

Releasing his astounded roommate, he went tearing across the campus to meet the carriage.

"What's happened to our staid and dignified president?" cried the Gutter Pup in wonder. "Is he crazy?"

" Oh, say, fellows," exclaimed the Kid, overcome by the humour of the situation, " who do you think that was? "

The carriage had now stopped before the Dickinson, and Turkey, arrived in time, was helping out a tall, slender figure in black. A light flashed over the group.

" Beauty's sister."

" No! "

" Yes."

" Impossible! "

" Beauty's sister it is," cried the Kid; " and the joke is, she's a stunner, a dream! "

" A dream! " piped up the inevitable Snookers. " Well, I guess! She's an all-round A-No. 1. Gee! I just got a glimpse of her at a theatre, and I tell you, boys, she's a paralyser."

But his remark ended on the air, for all, with a common impulse, had disappeared. Snookers, struck with the same thought, hastened to his room.

Ten minutes later they reappeared. Hickey, in a suit of pronounced checks, his trousers carefully turned up *à l'Anglais*, glanced approvingly at the array of manly fashion.

" And now, fellows," he said, pointing to the

Chapel, which Turkey was entering with Miss Sawtelle, "that traitor shall be punished. We'll guard
every entrance to Memorial, capture our friend,
'Chesterton V. Sawtelle (absent from bath),' relieve
him of that little dance-card, and then, Romans, to
the victors belong the spoils!"

The Kid having delayed over the choice between
a red-and-yellow necktie or one of simple purple, did
not appear until Hickey had stationed his forces.
Taking in the situation at a glance, he chuckled to
himself, and picking up a couple of books, started
for the entrance.

"Lucky it's Hungry and the Egghead," he said
to himself as he passed them and entered the Lower
Hall. "Hickey would have guessed the game."

He called Sawtelle from the second form, and,
slipping his arm through his, drew him down the corridor.

"Sawtelle," he said, "I want your sister's dance-
card. There's some mistake, and Turkey wants to
fix it up. Thanks; that's all. Oh, no, it isn't, either.
Turkey said he'd be over after supper to take your
sister to the debate, and that he had seats for the
Dramatic Club to-morrow. Don't forget all that.
So long! See you later."

In high feather at the success of this stratagem, he skipped downstairs, and avoiding Hickey, went to meet Turkey in the Chapel, where he was duly presented.

When Sawtelle emerged at length from the study-room, he was amazed at the spontaneity of his reception. He was no longer " Beauty " or " Apollo " or " Venus."

" Sawtelle, old man," they said to him, " I want to see you a moment."

" Chesterton, where have you been? "

" Old man, have you got anything to do? "

Each strove to draw him away from the others, and failing in this, accompanied him to the jigger-shop, where he was plied with substantial flattery, until having disposed of jiggers, soda, and éclairs, he cast one lingering glance at the tempting counters, and said with a twinkle in his ugly little eyes:

" And now, fellows, I guess my sister must be over at the house. Come around this afternoon, why don't you, and meet her? "—an invitation which was received with enthusiasm and much evident surprise.

When the Prom opened that evening, Beauty's sister made her entrée flanked by the smitten Turkey

and the languishing Hasbrouck, while the stricken
Kid brought up the rear, consoled by the responsibility of her fan. Five stags who had been lingering miserably in the shadow searching for something
daring and imaginative to lay at her feet, crowded
forward only to be stricken dumb at the splendour
of her toilette.

Beauty's sister, fresh from a Continental season,
was quite overwhelmed by the subtle adoration of the
famous Wash Simmons and of Egghead, that pattern
of elegance and *savoir-faire*—overwhelmed, but not
at all confused. Gradually under her deft manipu-
lation the power of speech returned to the stricken.
Then the rout began. The young ladies from city
and country finishing schools, still struggling with
their teens, were quite eclipsed by the gorgeous Pa-
risian toilette and the science of movement displayed
by the sister of Chesterton V. Sawtelle. The ordinary ethics of fair play were thrown to the winds.
Before the eyes of every one, Turkey held up the
worthless dance-card, and tore it into shreds. Only
the brave should deserve the fair. Little Smeed,
Poler Fox, and Snorky Green struggled in vain for
recognition, and retired crestfallen and defrauded,
to watch the scramble for each succeeding dance,

which had to be portioned among three and often four clamourers.

In fact, it became epidemic. They fell in love by blocks of five, even as they had sought the privileges of the measles. Each implored a memento to fix imperishably on his wall. The roses she wore consoled a dozen. The Gutter Pup obtained her fan; the Kid her handkerchief, a wonderful scented transparency. Glendenning and Hasbrouck brazenly divided the gloves, while Turkey, trembling at his own blurting audacity, was blown to the stars by permission to express in a letter certain delicate thoughts which stifle in the vulgar scramble of the ballroom.

When the last dance had been fought for, divided, and redivided, and the lights peremptorily suppressed, the stags *en masse* accompanied Beauty's sister to the Dickinson, where each separately pressed her hand and strove to give to his "Good-night" an accent which would be understood by her alone.

On that next morning that somehow always arises, Turkey and the Kid, envied by all, drove her to the station, listening mutely to her gay chatter, each plunged in melancholy, secretly wondering how she managed to conceal her feelings so well.

They escorted her to the car, and loaded her with

magazines and candies and flowers, and each succeeded in whispering in her ear a rapid, daring sentence, which she received from each with just the
proper encouragement. Then, imaginary Lucilles
and Marie Louises forgot, they drove back, heavy
of heart, and uncomprehending, viewing the land-
scape without joy or hope, suffering stoically as men
of eighteen should. Not a word was spoken until
from the last hill they caught the first glimmer of
the school. Then Turkey hoarsely, flicking the air
with the lash of the whip, said:

" Kid——"

" What? "

" That *was* a woman.

" A woman of the world, Turkey."

They left the carriage at the stable, and strolled
up to the jigger-shop, joining the group, all intent
on the coming baseball season; and gradually the
agony eased a bit. Presently a familiar little figure,
freckled and towheaded, sidled into the shop, and
stood with fists jammed in empty pockets, sniffing
the air for succour.

" Oh, you Beauty! oh, you astonishing Venus! "
cried the inevitable persecutor. Then from the
crowd Macnooder began to intone the familiar lines:

"His hair, it is a faded white,
　　His eye a watery blue;
　He has no buttons on his coat,
　　No shoe-strings in his shoe."

"Doc," said the Beauty, blushing sheepishly, "set me up to a jigger, will you? Go on, now!"

Then Macnooder, roaring, shouted back: "Not this year; next year—SISTER!"

THE GREAT BIG MAN

THE noon bell was about to ring, the one glorious spring note of that inexorable " Gym " bell that ruled the school with its iron tongue. For at noon, on the first liberating stroke, the long winter term died and the Easter vacation became a fact.

Inside Memorial Hall the impatient classes stirred nervously, counting off the minutes, sitting gingerly on the seat-edges for fear of wrinkling the carefully pressed suits or shifting solicitously the sharpened trousers in peril of a bagging at the knees. Heavens! how interminable the hour was, sitting there in a planked shirt and a fashion-high collar—and what a recitation! Would Easter ever begin, that long-coveted vacation when the growing boy, according to theory, goes home to rest from the fatiguing draining of his brain, but in reality returns exhausted by dinners, dances, and theatres, with perhaps a little touch of the measles to exchange with his neighbours. Even the masters droned through the perfunctory exercises, flunking the boys by twos and threes, by groups, by long rows, but without malice or emotion.

Outside, in the roadway, by the steps, waited a long, incongruous line of vehicles, scraped together from every stable in the countryside, forty-odd. A few buggies for nabobs in the Upper House, two-seated rigs (holding eight), country buckboards, excursion wagons to be filled according to capacity at twenty-five cents the trip, hacks from Trenton, and the regulation stage-coach—all piled high with bags and suitcases, waiting for the bell that would start them on the scramble for the Trenton station, five miles away. At the horses' heads the lazy ne-

groes lolled, drawing languid puffs from their cig-
arettes, unconcerned.

Suddenly the bell rang out, and the supine team-
sters, galvanising into life, jumped to their seats.
The next moment, down the steps, pell-mell, scrambling and scuffling, swarming over the carriages,
with joyful clamour, the school arrived. In an instant the first buggies were off, with whips franti-
cally plied, disputing at a gallop the race to Trenton.

Then the air was filled with shouts.

" Where's Butsey? "

" Oh, you, Red Dog! "

" Where's my bag? "

" Jump in! "

" Oh, we'll never get there! "

" Drive on! "

" Don't wait! "

" Where's Jack? "

" Hurry up, you loafer! "

" Hurry up, you butter-fingers! "

" Get in! "

" Pile in! "

" Haul him in! "

" We're off! "

" Hurrah! "

Wagon after wagon, crammed with joyful boy-hood, disappeared in a cloud of dust, while back returned a confused uproar of broken cheers, snatches of songs, with whoops and shrieks for more speed dominating the whole. The last load rollicked away to join the mad race, where far ahead a dozen buggies, with foam-flecked horses, vied with one another, their youthful jockeys waving their hats, hurling defiance back and forth, or shrieking with delight as each antagonist was caught and left behind.

The sounds of striving died away, the campus grew still once more. The few who had elected to wait until after luncheon scattered hurriedly about the circle and disappeared in the houses, to fling last armfuls into the already bursting trunks.

On top of Memorial steps the Great Big Man remained, solitary and marooned, gazing over the fields, down the road to Trenton, where still the rising dust-clouds showed the struggle toward vacation. He stood like a monument, gazing fixedly, struggling with all the might of his twelve years to conquer the awful feeling of homesickness that came to him. Homesickness—the very word was an anomaly: what home had he to go to? An orphan without ever having known his father, scarcely remembering his mother in the hazy reflections of years, little Joshua Tibbets had arrived at the school at the beginning of the winter term, to enter the shell,* and gradually pass through the forms in six or seven years.

The boys of the Dickinson, after a glance at his funny little body and his plaintive, doglike face, had baptised him the " Great Big Man " (Big Man for short), and had elected him the child of the house.

He had never known what homesickness was before. He had had a premonition of it, perhaps, from time to time during the last week, wondering a little in the classroom as each day Snorky Green, beside him, calculated the days until Easter, then the hours, then the minutes. He had watched him with an amused, uncomprehending interest. Why was he so anxious to be off? After all, he, the Big Man, found it a pleasant place, after the wearisome life from hotel to hotel. He liked the boys; they were kind to him, and looked after his moral and spiritual welfare with bluff but affectionate solicitude. It is true, one was always hungry, and only ten and a half hours' sleep was a refinement of cruelty un-

* The " shell " is the lowest class.

worthy of a great institution.   But it was pleasant running over to the jigger-shop and doing errands for giants like Reiter and Butcher Stevens, with the privileges of the commission.   He liked to be tumbled in the grass by the great tackle of the football eleven, or thrown gently from arm to arm like a medicine-ball, quits for the privileges of pommelling his big friends *ad libitum* and without fear of reprisals.   And then what a privilege to be allowed to run out on the field and fetch the noseguard or useless bandage, thrown down haphazard, with the confidence that he, the Big Man, was there to fetch and guard!   Then he was permitted to share their studies, to read slowly from handy, literal translations, his head cushioned on the Egghead's knee, while the lounging group swore genially at Pius Æneas or sympathised with Catiline.   He shagged elusive balls and paraded the bats at shoulder-arms.   He opened the mail, and sorted it, fetching the bag from Farnum's.   He was even allowed to stand treat to the mighty men of the house whenever the change in his pocket became too heavy for comfort.

In return he was taught to box, to wind tennis rackets, to blacken shoes, to crease trousers, and sew on the buttons of the house. Nothing was lacking to his complete happiness.

Then lately he had begun to realise that there was something else in the school life, outside it, but very much a part of it—vacation.

At first the idea of quitting such a fascinating life was quite incomprehensible to him. What gorging dinner-party could compare with the thrill of feasting at midnight on crackers and cheese, devilled ham, boned chicken, mince pie and root beer, by the light of a solitary candle, with the cracks of the doors and windows smothered with rugs and blankets, listening at every mouthful for the tread of the master that sometimes (oh, acme of delight!) actually passed unsuspectingly by the door?

Still, there was a joy in leaving all this. He began to notice it distinctly when the trunks were hauled from the cellar and the packing began. The packing—what a lark that had been! He had folded so many coats and trousers, carefully, in their creases, under Macnooder's generous instructions, and, perched on the edge of the banisters like a queer little marmoset, he had watched Wash Simmons throw great armfuls of assorted clothing into the trays and churn them into place with a baseball bat, while the Triumphant Egghead carefully built up his structure with nicety and tenderness. Only he, the Big Man, sworn to secrecy, knew what Hickey had surreptitiously inserted in the bottom of Egghead's trunk, and also what, from the depths of Wash's muddled clothing, would greet the fond mother or sister who did the unpacking; and every time he thought of it he laughed one of those laughs that pain. Then gleefully he had watched Macnooder stretching a strap until it burst with consequences dire, to the complete satisfaction of Hickey, Turkey, Wash, and the Egghead, who, embracing fondly on the top of another trunk, were assisting Butcher Stevens to close an impossible gap.

Yet into all this amusement a little strain of melancholy had stolen. Here was a sensation of which he was not part, an emotion he did not know. Still, his imagination did not seize it; he could not think of the halls quiet, with no familiar figures lolling out of the windows, or a campus unbrokenly green.

Now from his lonely eerie on Memorial steps, looking down the road to vacation, the Great Big Man suddenly understood—understood and felt. It was he who had gone away, not they. The school he loved was not with him, but roaring down to Trenton. No one had thought to invite him for a visit; but then, why should anyone?

"I'm only a runt, after all," he said, angrily, to himself. He stuck his fists deep in his pockets, and went down the steps like a soldier and across the campus chanting valorously the football slogan:

> Bill kicked,
> Dunham kicked.
> They both kicked together,
> But Bill kicked mighty hard.
> Flash ran,
> Charlie ran,
> Then Pennington lost her grip;
> She also lost the championship—
> Siss, boom, ah!

After all, he could sleep late; that was something. Then in four days the baseball squad would return, and there would be long afternoon practices to watch, lolling on the turf, with an occasional foul to retrieve. He would read The Count of Monte Cristo, and follow The Three Musketeers through a thousand far-off adventures, and Lorna Doone,— there was always the great John Ridd, bigger even than Turkey or the Waladoo Bird.

He arrived resolutely at the Dickinson, and started up the deserted stairs for his room. There was only one thing he feared; he did not want Mrs. Rogers, wife of the housemaster, to "mother" him. Anything but that! He was glad that after luncheon he would have to take his meals at the Lodge. That would avert embarrassing situations, for whatever his friends might think, he, the Great Big Man, was a runt in stature only.

To express fully the excessive gaiety he enjoyed, he tramped to his room, bawling out:

> "'Tis a jolly life we lead,
>   Care and sorrow we defy."

All at once a gruff voice spoke:
"My, what a lot of noise for a Great Big Man!"
The Big Man stopped thunderstruck. The voice came from Butcher Stevens' room. Cautiously he tiptoed down the hall and paused, with his funny little nose and eyes peering around the door-jamb. Sure enough, there was Butcher, and there were the Butcher's trunks and bags. What could it mean?

"I say," he began, according to etiquette, "is that you, Butcher?"

"Very much so, Big Man."

" What are you doing here? "

" The faculty, Big Man, desire my presence," said the Butcher, sarcastically. " They would like my expert advice on a few problems that are *per-plexing* them."

" Ah," said the Great Big Man, slowly. Then he understood. The Butcher had been caught two nights before returning by Sawtelle's window at a very late hour. He did not know exactly the facts because he had been told not to be too inquisitive, and he was accustomed to obeying instructions. Supposing the faculty should expel him! To the Big Man such a sentence meant the end of all things, something too horrible to contemplate. So he said, " Oh, Butcher, is it serious? "

" Rather, youngster; rather, I should say."

" What *will* the baseball team do? " said the Big Man, overwhelmed.

" That's what's worrying me," replied the crack first-baseman, gloomily. He rose and went to the window, where he stood beating a tattoo.

" You don't suppose Crazy Opdyke could cover the bag, do you? " said the Big Man.

" Lord, no! "

" How about Stubby? "

" Too short."

" They might do something with the Waladoo."

" Not for first; he can't stop anything below his knees."

" Then I don't see how we're going to beat Andover, Butcher."

" It does look bad."

" Do you think the faculty will—will——"

" Fire me? Pretty certain, youngster."

" Oh, Butcher!"

" Trouble is, they've got the goods on me—dead to rights."

" But does the Doctor know how it'll break up the nine? "

Butcher laughed loudly.

" He doesn't *ap*-preciate that, youngster."

" No," said the Big Man, reflectively. " They never do, do they? "

The luncheon bell rang, and they hurried down. The Big Man was overwhelmed by the discovery. If Butcher didn't cover first, how could they ever beat Andover and the Princeton freshmen? Even Hill School and Pennington might trounce them. He fell into a brown melancholy, until suddenly he caught the sympathetic glance of Mrs. Rogers on him, and for fear that she would think it was due to his own weakness, he began to chat volubly.

He had always been a little in awe of the Butcher. Not that the Butcher had not been friendly; but he was so blunt and rough and unbending that he rather repelled intimacy. He watched him covertly, admiring the bravado with which he pretended unconcern. It must be awful to be threatened with expulsion and actually to be expelled, to have your whole life ruined, once and forever,—The Big Man's heart was stirred. He said to himself that he had not been sympathetic enough, and he resolved to repair the error. So, luncheon over, he said with an appearance of carelessness:

"I say, old man, come on over to the jigger-shop. I'll set 'em up. I'm pretty flush, you know."

The Butcher looked down at the funny face and saw the kindly motive under the exaggerated bluffness. Being touched by it, he said gruffly:

"Well; come on, then, you old billionaire!"

The Big Man felt a great movement of sympathy in him for his big comrade. He would have liked to slip his little fist in the great brown hand and say something appropriate, only he could think of nothing appropriate. Then he remembered that among men there should be no letting down, no sentimentality. So he lounged along, squinting up at the Butcher and trying to copy his rolling gait.

At the jigger-shop, Al lifted his eyebrows in well-informed disapproval, saying curtly:

"What are you doing here, you Butcher, you?"

"Building up my constitution," said Stevens, with a frown. "I'm staying because I like it, of course. Lawrenceville is just lovely at Easter: spring birds and violets, and that sort of thing."

"You're a nice one," said Al, a baseball enthusiast. "Why couldn't you behave until after the Andover game?"

"Of course; but you needn't rub it in," replied the Butcher, staring at the floor. "Give me a double strawberry, and heave it over."

Al, seeing him not insensible, relented. He added another dab to the double jigger already delivered, and said, shoving over the glass:

"It's pretty hard luck on the team, Butcher. There's no one hereabouts can hold down the bag like you. Heard anything definite?"

"No."

"What do you think?"

"I'd hate to say."

"Is anyone doing anything?"

"Cap Kiefer is to see the Doctor to-night."

"I say, Butcher," said the Big Man, in sudden fear, "you won't go up to Andover and play against us, will you?"

"Against the school! Well, rather not!" said the Butcher, indignantly. Then he added: "No; if they fire me, I know what I'll do."

The Big Man wondered if he contemplated suicide; that must be the natural thing to do when one is expelled. He felt that he must keep near Butcher, close all the day. So he made bold to wander about with him, watching him with solicitude.

They stopped at Lalo's for a hot dog, and lingered at Bill Appleby's, where the Butcher mournfully tried the new mits and swung the bats with critical consideration. Then feeling hungry, they trudged up to Conover's for pancakes and syrup. Everywhere was the same feeling of dismay; what would become of the baseball nine? Then it suddenly dawned upon the Big Man that no one seemed to be sorry on the Butcher's account. He stopped with a pancake poised on his fork, looked about to make sure no one could hear him, and blurted out:

"I say, Butcher, it's not only on account of first base, you know; I'm darn sorry for *you*, honest!"

"Why, you profane little cuss," said the Butcher, frowning, "who told you to swear?"

"Don't make fun of me, Butcher," said the Great Big Man, feeling very little; "I meant it."

"Conover," said the Butcher, loudly, "more pancakes, and brown 'em!"

He, too, had been struck by the fact that in the general mourning there had been scant attention paid to his personal fortunes. He had prided himself on the fact that he was not susceptible to "feelings," that he neither gave nor asked for sympathy. He was older than his associates, but years had never reconciled him to Latin or Greek or, for that matter, to mathematics in simple or aggravated form. He had been the bully of his village out in northern Iowa, and when a stranger came, he trounced him first, and cemented the friendship afterward. He liked hard knocks, give and take. He liked the school because there was the long football season in the autumn, with the joy of battling, with every sinew of the body alert and the humming of cheers indistinctly heard, as he rammed through the yielding line. Then the spring meant long hours of romping over the smooth diamond, cutting down impossible hits, guarding first base like a bull-dog, pulling down the high ones, smothering the wild throws that came ripping along the ground, threatening to jump up against his eyes, throws that other fellows dodged. He was in the company of equals, of good fighters, like Charley De Soto, Hickey, Flash Condit, and Turkey, fellows it was a joy to fight beside. Also, it was good to feel that four hundred-odd wearers of the red and black put their trust in him, and that trust became very sacred to him. He played hard—very hard, but cleanly, because combat was the joy of his life to him. He broke other rules, not as a lark, but out of the same fierce desire for battle, to seek out danger wherever he could find it. He had been caught fair and square, and he knew that for that particular offence there was only one punishment. Yet he hoped against hope, suddenly realising what it would cost him to give up the great school where, however, he had never sought friendships or anything beyond the admiration of his mates.

The sympathy of the Big Man startled him, then made him uncomfortable. He had no intention of crying out, and he did not like or understand the new emotion. that rose in him as he wondered when his sentence would come.

" Well, youngster," he said, gruffly, " had enough? Have another round? "

" I've had enough," said the Big Man, heaving a sigh. " Let me treat, Butcher."

" Not to-day, youngster."

" Butcher, I—I'd like to. I'm awfully flush."

" Not to-day."

" Let's match for it."

"What!" said the Butcher, fiercely, " Don't let me hear any more of that talk. You've got to grow up first."

The Big Man, thus rebuked, acquiesced meekly. The two strolled back to the campus in silence.

" Suppose we have a catch," said the Big Man, tentatively.

" All right," said the Butcher, smiling.

Intrenched behind a gigantic mit, the Big Man strove valorously to hold the difficult balls. After a long period of this mitigated pleasure they sat down to rest. Then Cap Kiefer's stocky figure appeared around the Dickinson, and the Butcher went off for a long, solemn consultation.

The Big Man, thus relieved of responsibility, felt terribly alone. He went to his room and took down volume two of The Count of Monte Cristo, and stretched out on the window-seat. Somehow the stupendous adventures failed to enthrall him. It was still throughout the house. He caught himself listening for the patter of Hickey's shoes above, dancing a breakdown, or the rumble of Egghead's laugh down the hall, or a voice calling, "Who can lend me a pair of suspenders?"

And the window was empty. It seemed so strange to look up from the printed page and find no one in the Woodhull opposite, shaving painfully at the window, or lolling like himself over a novel, all the time keeping an eye on the life below. He could not jeer at Two Inches Brown and Crazy Opdyke practising curves, nor assure them that the Dickinson nine would just fatten on those easy ones. No one halloed from house to house, no voice below drawled out:

"Oh, you Great *Big Man!* Stick your head out of the window!"

There was no one to call across for the time o' day, or for just a nickel to buy stamps, or for the loan of a baseball glove, or a sweater, or a collar button, scissors, button-hook, or fifty and one articles that are never bought but borrowed.

The Great Big Man let The Count of Monte Cristo tumble unheeded on the floor, seized a tennis ball, and went across the campus to the esplanade of the Upper House, where for half an hour he bounced the ball against the rim of the ledge, a privilege that only a fourth former may enjoy. Tiring of this, he wandered down to the pond, where he skimmed innumerable flat stones until he had exhausted the attractions of this limited amusement.

"I—I'm getting homesick," he admitted finally. "I wish I had a dog—something living—around."

At supper-time he saw the Butcher again, and forgot his own loneliness in the concern he felt for his big friend. He remembered that the Butcher had said that if he were expelled he knew what he would do. What had he meant by that? Something terrible. He glanced up at the Butcher, and, being very apprehensive, made bold to ask:

"Butcher, I say, what does Cap think?"

"He hasn't seen the Doctor yet," said the Butcher. "He'll see him to-night. I guess I'll go over myself, just to leave a calling-card accordin' to *etiquette!*"

The Big Man kept his own counsel, but when the Butcher, after dinner, disappeared through the awful portal of Foundation House, he sat down in the dark under a distant tree to watch. In a short five minutes the Butcher reappeared, stood a moment undecided on the steps, stooped, picked up a handful of gravel, flung it into the air with a laugh, and started along the circle.

" Butcher ! "

" Hello, who's that ! "

" It's me, Butcher," said the Big Man, slipping his hand into the other's; " I—I wanted to know."

" You aren't going to get sentimental, are you, youngster? " said Stevens, disapprovingly.

" Please, Butcher," said the Great Big Man, pleadingly, " don't be cross with me! Is there any hope? "

" The Doctor won't see me, young one," said the Butcher, " but the *at*-mosphere was not encouraging."

" I'm sorry."

" Honest? "

" Honest."

" You *damn* little runt! "

They went hand in hand over to the chapel, where

they chose the back steps and settled down with the great walls at their back and plenty of gravel at their feet to fling aimlessly into the dusky night.

" Butcher? "

" Well, Big Man! "

" What will you do if—if they fire you? "

" Oh, lots of things. I'll go hunting for gold somewhere, or strike out for South America or Africa."

" Oh!" The Big Man was immensely relieved; but he added incredulously, " Then you'll give up football and baseball? "

" Looks that way."

" You won't mind? "

" Yes," said the Butcher, suddenly, "I will mind. I'll hate to leave the old school. I'd like to have one chance more."

" Why don't you tell the Doctor that? "

" Never! I don't cry out when I'm caught, youngster. I take my punishment."

" Yes," said the Big Man, reflecting. " That's right, I suppose; but, then, there's the team to think of, you know."

They sat for a long time in silence, broken suddenly by the Butcher's voice, not so gruff as usual.

" Say, Big Man—feeling sort of homesick? "

No answer.

" Just a bit? "

Still no answer. The Butcher looked down, and saw the Big Man struggling desperately to hold in the sobs.

" Here, none of that, youngster ! " he exclaimed in alarm. " Brace up, old man ! "

" I—I'm all right," said the Great Big Man with difficulty. " It's nothing."

The Butcher patted him on the shoulder, and then drew his arm around the little body. The Big Man put his head down and blubbered, just as though he had been a little fellow, while his companion sat perplexed, wondering what to do or say in the strange situation.

" So he's a little homesick, is he? " he said lamely.

" N-o-o," said the Great Big Man, " not just that; it's—it's all the fellows I miss."

The Butcher was silent. He, too, began to understand that feeling; only he, in his battling pride, resisted fiercely the weakness.

" You've got an uncle somewhere, haven't you, youngster? " he said gently. " Doesn't he look after you in vacation-time? "

"I don't miss *him*," replied the Big Man, shaking his head. Then he pulled himself together and said apologetically: "It's just being left behind that makes me such a damned cry-baby."

"Youngster," said the Butcher, sternly, "your language is *at*-rocious. Such words do not sound well in the mouth of a suckling of your size."

"I didn't mean to," said the Big Man, blushing.

"You must leave something to grow up for, young man," said the Butcher, profoundly. "Now tell me about that uncle of yours. I don't fancy his silhouette."

The Great Big Man, thus encouraged, poured out his lonely starved little heart, while the Butcher listened sympathetically, feeling a certain comfort in sitting with his arm around a little fellow-being. Not that he was sensible of giving much comfort; his comments, he felt, were certainly inadequate; nor did he measure in any way up to the situation.

"Now it's better, eh, Big Man?" he said at last when the little fellow had stopped. "Does you sort of good to talk things out."

"Oh, yes; thank you, Butcher."

"All right, then, youngster."

"All right. I say, you—you don't ever feel that way, do you—homesick, I mean?"

"Not much."

"You've got a home, haven't you?"

"Quite too much, young one. If they fire me, I'll keep away from there. Strike out for myself."

"Of course, then, it's different."

"Young one," said the Butcher, suddenly, "that's not quite honest. If I have to clear out of here, it will cut me up *con*-siderable."

"Honest?"

"A fact. I didn't know it before; but it will cut me up to strike out and leave all this behind. I want another chance; and do you know why?"

"Why?"

"I'd like to make friends. Oh, I haven't got any real friends, youngster; you needn't shake your head. It's my fault. I know it. You're the first mortal soul who cared what became of me. All the rest are thinking of the team."

"Now, Butcher——"

"Lord! don't think I'm crying out!" said the Butcher, in instant alarm. "It's all been up to me. Truth is, I've been too darned proud. But I'd like to get another whack at it."

"Perhaps you will, Butcher."

"No, no, there's no reason why I should." The Butcher sat solemnly a moment, flinging pebbles down into the dark tennis courts. Suddenly he said: "Look here, Big Man, I'm going to give you some good advice."

"All right, Butcher."

"And I want you to tuck it away in your thinker —savez? You're a nice kid now, a good sort, but you've got a lot of chances for being spoiled. Don't get fresh. Don't get a swelled head just because a lot of the older fellows let you play around. There's nothing so hateful in the sight of God or man as a fresh kid."

"You don't think——" began the Big Man in dismay.

"No; you're all right now. You're quiet, and don't tag around, and you're a good sort, darned if you aren't, and that's why I don't want to see you spoiled. Now a straight question: Do you smoke?"

"Why, that is—well, Butcher, I did try once a puff on Snookers' cigarette."

"You ought to be spanked!" said the Butcher, angrily. "And when I get hold of Snookers, I'll tan him. The idea of his letting you! Don't you monkey around tobacco yet a while. First of all, it's fresh, and second, you've got to *grow*. You want to make a team, don't you, while you're here?"

"O-o-oh!" said the Great Big Man with a long sigh.

"Then just stick to growing. 'Cause you've got work cut out for you there. Now I'm not preachin'; I'm saying that you want to fill out and grow up and do something. Harkee."

"All right."

"Cut out Snookers and that gang. Pick out the fellows that count, as you go along, and just remember this, if you forget the rest: if you want to put ducks in Tabby's bed or nail down his desk, do it because *you* want to do it, not because some other fellow wants you to do it. D'ye hear?"

"Yes, Butcher."

"Remember that, youngster; if I'd stuck to it, I'd kept out of a peck of trouble." He reflected a moment and added: "Then I'd study a little. It's not a bad thing, I guess, in the long run, and it gets the masters on your side. And now jump up, and we'll trot home."

The following night the Big Man, again under his tree, waited for the result of the conference that was going on inside Foundation House between the Doctor and the Butcher and Cap Kiefer. It was long, very long. The minutes went slowly, and it was very dark there, with hardly a light showing in the circle of houses that ordinarily seemed like a procession of lighted ferry-boats. After an interminable hour, the Butcher and Cap came out. He needed no word to tell what their attitudes showed only too plainly: the Butcher was expelled!

The Big Man waited until the two had passed into the night, and then, with a sudden resolve, went bravely to the doorbell and rang. Before he quite appreciated the audacity of his act, he found himself in the sanctum facing a much-perplexed head master.

" Doctor, I—I——" The Big Man stopped, overwhelmed by the awful majesty of the Doctor, on whose face still sat the grimness of the past conference.

" Well, Joshua, what's the matter?" said the head master, relaxing a bit before one of his favourites.

" Please, sir, I'm a little—a little embarrassed, I'm afraid," said the Great Big Man, desperately.

" Am I so terrible as all that?" said the Doctor, smiling.

" Yes, sir—you are," the Big Man replied frankly.

Then he said, plunging in, "Doctor, is the Butcher—is Stevens—are you going to—expel him?"

"That is my painful duty, Joshua," said the Doctor, frowning.

"Oh, Doctor," said the Big Man all in a breath, "you don't know—you're making a mistake."

"I am? Why, Joshua?"

"Because—you don't know. Because the Butcher won't tell you, he's too proud, sir; because he doesn't want to cry out, sir."

"What do you mean exactly?" said the Doctor in surprise. "Does Stevens know you're here?"

"Oh, Heavens, no, sir!" said the Big Man in horror. "And you must never tell him, sir; that would be too terrible."

"Joshua," said the Doctor, impressively, "I am expelling Stevens because he is just the influence I don't want boys of your age to come under."

"Oh, yes, sir," said the Big Man, "I know you think that, sir; but really, Doctor, that's where you are wrong; really you are, sir."

The Doctor saw there was something under the surface, and he encouraged the little fellow to talk. The Big Man, forgetting all fear in the seriousness of the situation, told the listening head master all the Butcher's conversation with him on the chapel steps the night before—told it simply and eloquently, with an ardour that bespoke absolute faith.   Then suddenly he stopped.

" That's all, sir," he said, frightened.

The Doctor rose and walked back and forth, troubled and perplexed.   There was no doubting the sincerity of the recital: it was a side of Stevens he had not guessed.   Finally he turned and rested his hand on the Big Man's shoulders.

" Thank you," he said ; " it does put another light on the question.   I'll think it over."

When, ten days later, the school came trickling home along the road from vacation, they saw, against all hope, the Butcher holding down first base, frolicking over the diamond in the old familiar way, and a great shout of joy and relief went up.   But how it had happened no one ever knew, least of all Cap and the Butcher, who had gone from Foundation House that night in settled despair.

To add to Butcher's mystification, the Doctor, in announcing his reprieve, had added:

" I've decided to make a change, Stevens.   I'm going to put Tibbetts in to room with you.   I place him in your charge.   I'm going to try a little responsibility on you."

THE POLITICAL EDUCATION OF MR. BALDWIN

IF Hickey had not been woefully weak in mathematics the famous Fed. and anti-Fed. riots would probably never have happened. But as revolutions turn on minor axes, Hickey, who could follow a football like a hound, could not for the life of him trace X, the unknown factor, through the hedges of the simplest equation.

It was, therefore, with feelings of the acutest interest that he waited, in the upper corridor of Memorial Hall, on the opening morning of the spring term, for the appearance of Mr. Baldwin, the new recruit to the mathematics department. The Hall was choked with old boys chattering over the doings of the Easter vacation, calling back and forth, punching one another affectionately or critically examining the returning stragglers.

"His name is Ernest Garrison Baldwin," said the Gutter Pup. "Just graduated, full of honours and that sort of thing."

"He ought to be easy," said Crazy Opdyke, hopefully.

"These mathematical sharks are always fancy markers," interposed Macnooder.

"If I'm stuck in the first row," said the Egghead gloomily, "it's all up—I never could do anything with figures."

"If we want short lessons," said Hickey, waking out of his reverie, "we've all got to flunk in the beginning."

At this Machiavellian analysis there was a chorus of assent.

"Sure."

"Hickey's the boy!"

"Red Dog and Poler Fox have got to be kept down."

"We're not pack-horses."

"Say, is he green?"

" Sure—never taught before."

" Cheese it—he's coming."

The group stood aside, intent on the arrival of the new adversary. They saw a stiff young man, already bald, with a set, affable manner and a pervading smile of cordiality, who entered the classroom with a confident step, after a nodded:

" Ah, boys—good-morning."

The class filed in, eyeing the natural enemy closely for the first indications of value to aid them in the approaching conflicts.

" He's awfully serious," said the Egghead to his neighbour.

" He'll try to drive us," replied Macnooder, with instinctive resentment.

Hickey said nothing, absorbed in contemplation of a momentous question—how would the new master hear recitations? To solve a master's system is to be prepared in advance, and with the exception of the Roman's there was not a system which he had not solved. Popular masters, like Pa Dater, called you up every third day, which is eminently just and conducive to a high standard of scholarship. The Muffin Head, in stealthy craftiness, had a way of calling you up twice in succession after you had flunked and were expecting a brief period of immunity; but this system once solved gave ample opportunity to redeem yourself. The Doctor, wiser than the rest, wrote each name on a card, shuffled the pack and called for a recitation according to chance —but even the Doctor left the pack on his desk, nor counted the cards as all careful players should. Other masters, like Tapping and Baronson, trusted to their intuitions, seizing upon the boy whose countenance betrayed a lurking apprehension. Hickey took kindly to this method and had thrived amazingly, by sudden flagrant inattentions or noticeable gazing out of the windows, which invariably procured him a staccato summons to recite just as the recitation neared the limited portion he had studied.

So Hickey sat, examining Mr. Baldwin, and speculating into which classification he would fall.

" Now, boys," said Mr. Baldwin, with an expanding smile, " we're beginning the new term. I hope you'll like me—I know I shall like you. I'm quite a boy myself—quite a boy, you know. Now I'm going ahead on a new principle. I'm going to assume that you all take an interest in your work [the class sat up]. I'm going to assume that you look upon life with seriousness and purpose. I'm going to assume that you realise the sacrifices your parents are making to afford you an education. I'm not here as a taskmaster. I'm here to help you, as your friend, as your companion—as an older brother—that's it, as an older brother. I hope our interest in one another will not be limited to this classroom."

Hickey and the Egghead, who had prominently installed themselves in the front seats, led the applause with serious, responsive faces. Mr. Baldwin acknowledged it, noticing pleasantly the leaders of the demonstration.

Then he rapped for order and began to call the roll, seating the boys alphabetically. He ran rapidly through the F's, the G's and H's and, pausing, inquired:

" Are there any J's in the class? "

At this excruciatingly witty remark, which every master annually blunders upon, the waiting class roared in unison, while Hinsdale was forced to slap Hickey mercilessly on the back to save him from violent hysterics.

Mr. Baldwin, who suddenly perceived he had made a pun, hastily assumed a roguish expression and allowed a considerable moment for the laughter to die away. The session ended in a gale of cordiality.

Hickey and the Egghead paid a visit that afternoon to the Griswold, to make the new arrival feel quite at home.

"Ah, boys," said Mr. Baldwin, with a wringing hand-shake, "this is very friendly of you, very friendly."

"Mr. Baldwin," said Hickey seriously, "we were very much interested in what you said to us this morning."

"Indeed," said Baldwin, gratified. "Well, that pleases me very much. And I am glad to see that you take me at my word, and I hope you will drop in often. There are lots of things I want to talk over with you."

"Yes, sir," said the Egghead. "It's very kind of you."

"Not at all," said Baldwin, with a wave of his hand. "My theory is that a master should be your companion, and I have one or two ideas about education I am anxious to have my boys interested in. Now, for instance, take politics; what do you know about politics?"

"Why, nothing," said Hickey in acquiescent surprise.

"And yet that is the most vital thing you will

have to face as men. Here's a great national election approaching, and yet, I am certain not one in four hundred of you has any clear conception of the political system."

"That's so, Egghead," said Hickey, nodding impressively at his companion. "It *is* so."

"I have a scheme I'm going to talk over with you," continued Baldwin, "and I want your advice. Sit down; make yourselves comfortable."

Later in the afternoon Mr. Baronson, Baldwin's superior in the Griswold, dropped in with a friendly inquiry. Young Mr. Baldwin was gazing out of the window in indulgent amusement. Mr. Baronson, following his gaze, beheld, in the far campus, Hickey and Egghead rolling over each other like two trick bears.

"Well, Baldwin, how goes it?" said Baronson genially.

"Splendidly. The boys are more than friendly. We shall get on famously."

"'*Danaos timeo et dona ferentes,*'" said Baronson shrewdly.

"Oh ——" Baldwin objected.

"Yes, yes—I'm an old fogy—old style," said Baronson, cutting in, "but it's based on good scientific researches, Baldwin. I just dropped in for a hint or two, which you won't pay attention to— never mind. When you've lived with the young human animal as long as I have, you won't have any illusions. He doesn't want to be enlightened. He hasn't the slightest desire to be educated. He isn't educated. He never will be. His memory simply *detains* for a short while, a larger and larger number of facts—Latin, Greek, history, mathematics, it's all the same—facts, nothing but facts. He remembers when he is compelled to, but he is supremely bored by the performance. All he wants is to grow, to play and to get into sufficient mischief. My dear fellow, treat him as a splendid young savage, who breaks a rule for the joy of matching his wits against yours, and don't take him seriously, as you are in danger of doing. Don't let him take you seriously or he will lead you to a cropper."

Ernest Garrison Baldwin did not deign to reply— the voice of the older generation, of course! He was of the new, he would replace old prejudices with new methods. There were a great many things in the world he intended to change—among others this whole antagonistic spirit of education. So he remained silent, and looked very dignified.

Baronson studied him, saw the workings of his mind, and smiled.

" Never were at boarding-school, were you? " he asked.

" No," said Baldwin, drily.

Baronson gave a glance at the study, remarked the advanced note in the shelves, and went to the door.

" After all," he said, with his hand on the knob, " the first year, Baldwin, we learn more than we teach."

" Gee! I think it's an awful bore," said the Gutter Pup.

" I don't see it either," said the Egghead.

" Who started it? " asked Turkey Reiter.

" Hickey and Elder Brother Baldwin," said the Egghead. " Hickey's improving his stand."

" Hickey, boy," said Butcher Stevens, professionally, " you're consorting with awful low company."

" Hickey, you are getting to be a greasy grind," said the Gutter Pup.

" I am, am I," said Hickey indignantly. " I'd like to know if I'm not a patriot. I'd like to know if I'm not responsible for the atmosphere of brotherly love and the dove of peace that floats around Baldwin's classroom. I'd like to know if I'm not responsible for his calling us up alphabetically, regular order, every other day, no suspicion, perfect trust—mutual confidence. Am I right?"

"You are right, Hickey, you are right," said Turkey apologetically. "The binomial theorem is a delight and a joy, when, as you say, the master has mutual trust in the scholar. But where in blazes, Hickey, did you get this political shindy into your thinker?"

"It's Elder Brother's theory of education," said Hickey carefully, "*one* of his theories. Elder Brother is very much distressed at the ignorance, the political ignorance, of the modern boy. Brother is right."

"Come off," said the Egghead, glancing at him suspiciously, but Hickey maintained a serious face.

"What's up?" said Macnooder, sauntering over to the crowd on the lawn.

"Hickey's fixed up a plan with Brotherly Love to have a political campaign," said the Gutter Pup, "and is trying to rouse our enthusiasm."

"A campaign here in the school, in the Lawrenceville School, John C. Green Foundation!" said Macnooder incredulously.

" The same! "

" No? I won't believe it. It's a dream—it's a beautiful, satisfying dream," said Macnooder, shaking his head. " A political campaign in school; Hickey, my bounding boy, I see your cunning hand! "

" Now Doc's gone nutty," said the unimaginative Egghead. " What the deuce do you see in it? "

" Hickey, you old, rambunctious, foxy, prodigious Hickey, I knew something was brewing," said Doc, not deigning to notice the Egghead. " You have been quiet, most quiet of late. Hickey, how did you do it? "

" Sympathy, Doc," said Hickey blandly. " I've been most sympathetic with Elder Brother, sympathetic and most encouraging. Sympathy is a beautiful thing, Doc, beautiful and rare."

" Hickey, don't torture me with curiosity," said Doc. " Where are we at? "

" At the present moment, Brother is asking the Doctor for permission to launch the campaign, and the sympathetic, popular and serious Hickey Hicks is proceeding to select a preliminary conference committee."

. " And what then? " said Turkey, with sudden interest.

" What then? " said Hickey. " Bonfires, parades, stump speeches, proclamations, et cetera, et ceteray."

" Oh, Hickey," said the now enthusiastic Gutter Pup, " do you think the Doctor ever will permit it? "

" What's the use of getting excited? " said the Egghead contemptuously. " You don't fancy for a moment, do you, there's a chance of fooling the Doctor? "

" Sure, Egghead's right," said Butcher Stevens; " you won't get the Doctor to bite. Baldwin is green, but the Doctor is quite ripe, thank you! "

Even Macnooder looked dubiously at Hickey, who assumed an air of superhuman wisdom and answered:

" I have two chances, Baldwin and the De-coy Ducks! "

" The what? "

" Decoy Ducks; the committee that will confer to-morrow afternoon with the Doctor."

Turkey emitted a long, admiring whistle.

" I have given the matter thought — serious thought, as Baldwin would say," said Hickey. " The following collection of Archangels and young High Markers will be rounded up for the Doctor's inspection to-morrow."

" As Decoy Ducks? "

" As Decoy Ducks, you intelligent Turkey. High Markers: Red Dog, Poler Fox, Biddy Hampton and Ginger Pop Rooker, Wash Simmons—the Doctor would feed out of Wash's hand—Crazy Opdyke—he reads Greek like Jules Verne. Everything must be done to make this a strictly ed-u-cational affair. Now to demonstrate that it has the sanction of the religious element of this community the following notorious and flagrant Archangels will qualify: Halo Brown, Pink Rabbit, Parson Eddy, the Saphead and the Coffee Cooler—the Doctor is real affectionate with the Coffee Cooler."

" What a beoo-ti-ful bunch! " said the Gutter Pup rapturously.

" It is," said Hickey, proudly; " the Doctor would let any one of them correct his own examination papers and raise the mark afterward on the ground of overconscientiousness."

" Well, where's the fun? " said the Egghead obstinately. " If Crazy Opdyke and that bunch is to run the campaign, where do we come in? "

" There will be a small preliminary representation of professional politicians," said Hickey, smiling. " very small at present, limited to the handsome and popular Hickey Hicks, who will represent the large

body of professional politicians who will be detained
at home by hard work and serious application,
but——"

"But what?" said Macnooder.

"But who will find time to ac-tively assist this
quiet, orderly campaign of education, *after* their
presence will not be misunderstood!"

At half-past one the next day, the Doctor, sympathetically inclined by the enthusiastic, if inexperienced, Mr. Baldwin, received the Decoy Ducks in his
study at Foundation House.

The Doctor, while interested, had not been convinced, and had expressed a desire to know into whose
guidance the nurturing of such a tender plant had
been intrusted. As the impressive gathering defiled
before him, his instinctive caution vanished, his
glance warmed with satisfaction, and assuming the
genial and conversational attitude he reserved for
his favourites, he began:

"Well, boys, this appears to be a responsible gathering, an unusually responsible one. It is gratifying
to see you approaching such subjects with serious
purpose and earnestness. It is gratifying that the
leaders of this school" (here his glance rested fondly

on Wash Simmons, Crazy Opdyke and the Coffee Cooler, prominently placed) " that the earnest, purposeful boys show this interest in the political welfare of the nation.   Mr. Baldwin's plan seems to me to be a most excellent one.   I am in hearty accord with its motive.   We cannot begin too soon to interest the youth, the intelligent, serious youth of our country in honest government and clean political methods." (Hickey, in noble effacement by the window-seat, here gazed dreamily over the campus to the red circle of houses.)   " Much can be accomplished from the earnest and purposeful pursuit of this instructive experiment.   The experiment should be educational in the largest sense ; the more I study it the more worthy it appears.   I should not be surprised if your experiment should attract the consideration of the educational world.   Mr. Baldwin, it gives me pleasure to express to you my thanks and my gratification for the authorship of so worthy an undertaking.   I will leave you to a discussion of the necessary details."

" Well, boys," said Baldwin briskly, " let me briefly outline the plan agreed upon.   The election shall be for a school council, before which legislation affecting the interests of the school shall come.   Each of the f · forms shall elect two repr···· · ··· ···· ·uch of the ten houses shall elect one representative, making a deliberative body of eighteen. In view of the fact that the approaching national election might inject unnecessary bitterness if the election should be on national issues, we have decided, on the very excellent suggestion of Hicks, who has indeed given many valuable suggestions " (Hickey looked preternaturally solemn), " to have the election on a matter of school policy, and have settled upon the athletic finances as an issue of sufficient interest and yet one that can be calmly and orderly discussed. At present, the management of the athletic finances is in the hands of selected officers from the fourth form. The issue, then, is whether this method shall be continued or whether a member of the faculty shall administer the finances. I should suggest Federalists and Anti-Federalists as names for the parties you will form. One week will be given to campaigning and the election will take place according to the Australian ballot system. Now, boys, I wish you success. You will acquire a taste for public combat and a facility in the necessary art of politics that will nurture in you a desire to enter public life, to take your part in the fight for honest politics, clear methods, independent thinking, and will make you foes

of intimidation, bribery, cheating and that dema-
goguery that is the despair of our present system.
At present you may be indifferent, a little bored, perhaps, at this experiment, but you will like it—I am
sure you will like it. I prophesy it will interest you
once you get started."

Hickey lingered after the meeting to explain that
the duties incident to the organising of such an important undertaking had unfortunately deprived him
of the time necessary to prepare his advanced
algebra.

"Well, that is a little matter we'll overlook,
Hicks," said the enthusiast genially. "I congratulate you on your selection, an admirable committee,
one that inspires confidence. Keep me in touch with
developments and call on me for advice at any time."

"Yes, indeed, sir."

"Good luck."

"Thank you, sir."

A half hour later Hickey announced the addition
of the following professional politicians: Tough
McCarthy, Doc Macnooder, The Triumphant Egghead, Slugger Jones, Turkey Reiter, Cheyenne Baxter, Jock Hasbrouck, Butcher Stevens, Rock Bemis
and B t Greer.

The reinforced committee then met, divided equitably, and having tossed for sides, announced their organisation, as follows:

FEDERALIST PARTY
Chairman: THE HON. TOUGH MCCARTHY
Vice-Chairman: THE HON. GINGER POP ROOKER

ANTI-FEDERALIST PARTY
Chairman: HON. CHEYENNE BAXTER
Vice-Chairman: HON. HICKEY HICKS

The school was at first apathetic, then mildly interested. The scheme was examined with suspicion as perhaps being a veiled attempt of the faculty to increase the already outrageous taxes on the mind. It looked prosy enough at first glance—perhaps an attempt to revive the interest in debating and so to be fiercely resisted.

For an hour the great campaign for political education hung fire and then suddenly it began to catch on. A few leading imaginations had seen the latent possibilities. In another hour apathy had disappeared and every house was discussing the momentous question whether to go Fed or Anti-Fed.

The executive committee of the Federalist party met immediately, on a call from the Honourable

Cheyenne Baxter, in the Triumphant Egghead's rooms for organisation and conference.

" We've got the short end of it, all right, all right," said Butcher Stevens gloomily. " The idea of our standing up for the faculty."

" That's right, Cheyenne," said Turkey, shaking his head. " We'll be left high and dry."

" We won't carry any house outside the Dickinson and the Woodhull," said Slugger Jones.

" I'd like to make a suggestion," said Crazy Opdyke.

" We've got to plan two campaigns," said Cheyenne, " one for the election from the forms and one for the control of the houses. Let's take up the forms—the fourth form will go solidly against us."

" Sure," said Doc Macnooder, " because if we win they lose control of the finances."

" I have a suggestion," said Crazy Opdyke for the second time.

" Now," said Cheyenne, " we've got to make this a matter of the school against the fourth form, and it oughtn't to be so hard, either. Now, how're we going to do it? First, what have we got?"

" The Dickinson and the Woodhull," said Hickey.

" Yes, we can be sure of those, but that's all.

Now, those Feds, with Jock Hasbrouck and Tough McCarthy, will swing the Kennedy and the Griswold."

" The Davis House will be against us," said Macnooder, with conviction. " They're just aching to get back at the Dickinson."

" That's so," said Turkey. " They're still sore because we won the football championship."

" The Davis will pull the Rouse House with it," said Hickey gloomily. " They're forty in the Davis and only twelve in the Rouse. The Davis would mangle them if they ever dared go our way."

" We've got to counteract that by getting the Green," said Cheyenne. " They're only ten there, but it makes a vote. The fight'll be in the Hamill and the Cleve."

" The Cleve is sore on us," said Turkey of the Dickinson, " because we swiped the ice cream last year for their commencement dinner."

" I've got an idea," said Crazy Opdyke, trying to be heard.

" Shut up, Crazy," said Doc. " You've served your purpose; you're a Decoy Duck and nothing else."

" Harmony!" said Cheyenne warningly. " The

way to get the Green is to give Butsey White, down there, the nomination from the second form, if he'll swing the house."

"And put up Bronc Andrews in the Hamill," added Macnooder.

"Where do I come in?" said Crazy Opdyke, who had aspirations.

"You subordinate yourself to the success of your party," said Cheyenne.

"The devil I do," said Opdyke. "If you think I'm a negro delegate, you've got another think coming. I may be a Decoy Duck, but either I'm made chairman of a Finance Committee or I lead a bolt right out of this convention."

"A Finance Committee?" said Butcher Stevens, mystified.

"Sure," said Cheyenne Baxter. "That's most important."

"I'll take that myself, then," said Macnooder aggressively. "I'd like to know what claim Crazy's got to a position of trust and responsibility."

"Claim or no claim," said Opdyke, pulling his hat over his eyes and tilting back, "either I handle the funds of this here campaign or the Anti-Federalist party begins to split."

" Shall a half-plucked rooster from the Cleve House hold up this convention? " said Wash Simmons militantly. " If we're going to be black-jacked by every squid that comes down the road, *I'm* going to get out."

" I have spoken," said Crazy.

" So have I."

" Gentlemen, gentlemen," protested the Honourable Cheyenne Baxter, " we must have harmony."

" Rats! " said Opdyke. " I demand a vote."

" I insist upon it," said Wash.

The vote was taken and Macnooder was declared chairman of the Finance Committee. Crazy Opdyke arose and made them a profound bow.

"Gentlemen, I have the honour of bidding you farewell," he said, loftily. " The voice of freedom has been stifled. This great party is in the hands of commercial interests and private privilege. This is nothing but a Dickinson House sinecure. I retire, I withdraw, I shake the dust from my feet. I depart, but I shall not sleep, I shall not rest, I shall neither forget nor forgive. Remember, gentlemen of the Anti-Federalist party, this hour, and when in the stillness of the night you hear the swish of the poisoned arrow, the swirl of the tomahawk, the thud of the secret stone, pause and say to yourself, ' Crazy Opdyke done it ! ' "

" It is unfortunate," said Cheyenne, when Crazy had departed, " most unfortunate, but that's politics."

" Crazy has no influence," said Wash, contemptuously.

" He has our secrets," said Cheyenne gloomily.

" Let's get to work," said Macnooder. " You can bet Tough McCarthy's on the job; his father's an alderman."

At six o'clock the campaign was off with a rush. At seven the head master, all unsuspecting, stepped out from Foundation House, cast one fond glance at the familiar school, reposing peacefuly in the twilight, and departed to carry the message of increased liberty in primary education to a waiting conference at Boston. Shortly after, a delegation of the school faculty, who had just learned of the prospective campaign, hurried over in amazed, indignant and incredulous protest. They missed the head master by ten minutes — but ten minutes make history.

" Jiminy crickets ! "

" Suffering Moses ! "

" Call Hickey! "

" Tell Hickey! "

" Hickey, stick your head out of the window! "

Hickey, slumbering peacefully, in that choicest period between the rising bell and breakfast, leaped to the middle of the floor at the uproar that suddenly resounded through the Dickinson.

He thrust his head out of the window and beheld from the upper stories of the Griswold an immense white sheet sagging in the breeze, displaying in crude red-flannel letters the following device:

> NO APRON-STRINGS FOR US
> THE FEDERAL PARTY
> WILL FIGHT TO THE END
> FACULTY USURPATION

Hardly had his blinking eyes become accustomed to the sight when a fresh uproar broke out on the other side of the Dickinson.

" Hully Gee! "

" Look at the Kennedy! "

" Great cats and little kittens! "

" Snakes alive! "

" Look at the Kennedy, will you! "

" Hickey, oh you, Hickey! "

At the sound of Macnooder's voice in distress, Hickey realised the situation was serious and rushed across the hall. He found Macnooder with stern and belligerent gaze fixed out of the window. From the Kennedy House another banner insolently displayed this amazing proclamation:

DOWN WITH THE GOO-GOOS
LAWRENCEVILLE SHALL NOT BE
A KINDERGARTEN.
RALLY TO THE FEDERALISTS AND
DOWN THE DICKINSON GOO-GOOS

Hickey looked at Macnooder. Macnooder looked at Hickey.

" Goo-Goo," said Hickey, grieved.

" Goo-Goo," repeated Doc sadly. " Goo-Goo and Apron-strings. Hickey, my boy, we have got to be up and doing."

" Doc," said Hickey, " that's Tough McCarthy's work. We never ought to have let him get away from us."

" Hickey, we must nail the lie," said Doc solemnly.

" The Executive Committee of the Anti-Fed party will meet in my rooms," said Hickey determinedly,

" directly after first recitation. We have been caught napping by a gang of ballot stuffers, but we will come back—Doc, we *will* come back!"

The Executive Committee met with stern and angry resolve, like battling football players between the halves of a desperate game.

" Fellows," said Hickey, " while we have slept the enemy has been busy. We are muts, and the original pie-faced mut is yours truly."

" No, Hickey, if there's going to be a competition for muts," said Cheyenne Baxter, " I'm the blue ribbon."

" Before we bestow any more bouquets," said Macnooder sarcastically, " let's examine the situation. Let's see the worst. The Feds have the jump on us. They've raised the cry of 'Apron-strings' on us, and it's going to be a mighty hard one to meet."

" We'll never answer it," said the gloomy Egghead; " we're beaten now. It's a rotten issue and a rotten game."

At this moment the Gutter Pup rushed in like a white fuzzy dog, his eyes bulging with importance as he delivered the bombshell, that Crazy Opdyke had organised a Mugwump party and carried the Cleve House for it.

" No."

" A Mugwump party! "

" What the deuce is he up to? "

" Order," said Hickey, stilling the tumult with a shoe vigorously applied to a wash-basin. " This meeting is not a bunch of undertakers. We are here to save the party."

" Hickey's right," said Turkey; " let's get down to business."

" First," said Hickey, " let's have reports. What has Treasurer Macnooder to report? "

The Mark Hanna of the campaign rose, tightened his belt, adjusted his glasses, and announced amid cheers that the Finance Committee had to report sixty-two dollars and forty cents in promissory notes, twelve dollars and thirty-eight cents in cash, three tennis rackets, two jerseys, one dozen caps, a bull's-eye lantern (loaned) and a Flobert rifle.

" We can always have a banquet, even if we're beaten," said the Triumphant Egghead. The gloom began to dissipate.

" What has the Honourable Gutter Pup to report? " said Cheyenne Baxter.

The Rocky Mountain Gazelle proudly announced the establishment of a thorough system of espionage, through the corrupting of Mr. Klondike Jackson, the coloured gentleman who waited on the table at the Kennedy, and Mr. Alcibiades Bonaparte, who shook up the beds at the Griswold. He likewise reported that young Muskrat Foster, who was not overpopular at the Davis House, had perceived the great truths of Anti-Federalism. He then presented a bill of two dollars and forty-five cents for the corrupting of the Messrs. Jackson and Bonaparte, with an addition of fifty cents for the further contaminating of young Muskrat Foster.

"The Honourable Wash Simmons will report," said Cheyenne Baxter.

"Fellows," said Wash, "I ain't no silver-tongued orator, and all I've got to say is that Butsey White, down at the Green House, is most sensible to the honour of representing this great and glorious party of moral ideas, as congressman from the second form, but——"

"But what?" said Slugger Jones.

"But he kind of fears that the other members of the Green House aren't quite up on Anti-Federalism, and he reckons it will take quite a little literature to educate them."

"Literature?" said Cheyenne, mystified.

" About eight volumes," said Wash. " Eight green-backed pieces of *literature!* "

" The robber! "

" Why, that's corruption."

" Gentlemen," said Cheyenne, rapping for order, " the question is, does he get the literature? Ayes or noes."

" I protest," interrupted Hickey. " Remember, gents, this is a campaign for clean politics. We will not buy votes, no! we will only encourage local enterprises. The Green is trying to fit themselves out for the baseball season. I suggest contributing toward a catcher's mit and a mask, and letting it go at that."

On the announcement of a unanimous vote, the Honourable Wash Simmons departed to encourage local enterprises.

" And now, fellows," said Hickey, " we come to the serious proposition—the real business of the meeting. We have got to treat with Crazy Opdyke."

" Never! "

" Macnooder must sacrifice himself," said Hickey. " Am I right, Cheyenne? "

" You are," said Cheyenne. " The campaign has

reached a serious stage. The Upper, the Kennedy, the Griswold, the Davis, are already Fed; the Rouse will go next. Even if we get the Green, we're lost if the Cleve goes against us, and Crazy is just holding out to make terms."

"We have misjudged Crazy," said Hickey; "his record was against him, but we have misjudged him. He's been the only live one in the bunch. Now we've got to meet his terms.

The door opened and Crazy Opdyke sauntered in.

"Hello, fellows," he drawled. "How's the campaign going? Are you satisfied with your progress?" He stretched languidly into an armchair. "Am I still welcome in the home of great moral ideas?"

"Crazy, our feelings for you are both of sorrow and of affection," said Cheyenne, conciliatingly. "You certainly are a boss politician. What's this new wrinkle of yours over in the Cleve?"

"I've been amusing myself," said Crazy with a drawl, "organising the Mugwumps, the intelligent and independent vote, the balance of power, you know, the party that doesn't heel to any boss, but votes according to its, to its——"

"To its what, Crazy?" said Hickey, gently.

" To its conscience," replied Crazy firmly. " To its conscience, when its conscience is intelligently approached."

" Oh, you're for sale, are you? " said Turkey aggressively.

" No, Turkey, no-o-o! And yet we've organised the Blocks of Five Marching Club; rather significant, eh? "

" Well, what's your game; what have you come for? "

" Oh, just to be friendly," said Crazy, rising languidly.

" Stop," said Hickey. " Sit down. Let's have a few words."

Crazy slouched back, sunk into the armchair and assumed a listening position.

" Crazy," said Hickey, " we've made a mistake. We didn't know you. You are the surprise of the campaign. We apologise. We are merely amateurs; you are the only original, professional politician."

" This is very gratifying," said Crazy, without a blush.

" Crazy, from this moment," said Hickey, firmly, " you are the treasurer of the Campaign Committee, and we're listening for any words of wisdom you have ready to uncork."

"No, Hickey, no," said Crazy, rising amid general dismay, "I no longer hanker to be a treasurer. It was just a passing fancy. Independence is better and more profitable; I appreciate your kind offer, I do appreciate it, Hickey, but I'm a Mugwump; I couldn't wear a dog-collar, I couldn't!"

"Sit down again, Crazy," said Hickey, persuasively; "sit down. It's a pleasure to talk with you. You're right; your independent and intelligent nature would be thrown away in a matter of books and figures. We've been looking round for a fearless, upright, popular and eloquent figure to stand for the Cleve, and, Crazy, we're just aching to have you step up into the frame."

"Hickey, you mistake me, you mistake me and my motives," said Crazy, sadly. "My soul does not hanker for personal glorification or the flattery of the multitude. I'm a child of nature, Hickey, and my ambitions are few and simple."

"It's right to have ambitions, Crazy," said Hickey, soothingly, "and they don't need to be few or simple. We regret that we cannot honour your eminent qualities as we wish to, but we still have hopes, Crazy, that we may have the benefit of your guiding hand."

"Guiding hand?" said Crazy, looking at the ceiling.

"Exactly," said Hickey, magnanimously; "in fact, I realise how unworthy I am to fill the great position of trust and responsibility of vice-chairman of this committee, and I long to see it in the hands——"

"I thought you said guiding hand," said Crazy, interrupting.

The assembled committee looked in amazement at Crazy. Then the storm broke out.

"Why, you insolent, impudent pup!"

"Do you think we'll make you chairman?"

"Kick him out!"

"Rough-house!"

"Order!" cried Cheyenne. "Crazy, out with it. You want to be chairman, don't you?"

"Have I made any demands?" said Crazy, coolly.

"Come now—yes or no!"

"Are you handing it to me?"

A fresh storm of indignation was interrupted by the sudden tumultuous reappearance of Wash Simmons, shouting:

"Fellows, Butsey White and the Green have sold out to the Mugwumps!"

Crazy Opdyke sat down again.

A long silence succeeded.   Then Cheyenne Baxter, mutely interrogating every glance, rose and said:

"Crazy, you win.   The chairmanship is yours. Will you take it on a silver platter or with a bouquet of roses?"

That evening, when Hickey went to report to Ernest Garrison Baldwin, he found that civic reformer in a somewhat perturbed condition.

"I'm afraid, Hicks," he said dubiously, "that the campaign is getting a wrong emphasis.   It seems to me that those Federalist banners are not only in questionable taste, but show a frivolous and trifling attitude toward this great opportunity."

"It's just the humour of the campaign, sir," said Hickey reassuringly; "I wouldn't take them seriously."

"Another thing, Hicks; I'm rather surprised that the management of the campaign does not seem to be in the hands of the very representative committee you originally selected."

"Yes, sir," said Hickey; "we realise that; but we're making a change in our party at least which will please you. Opdyke is going to take control."

"Indeed! That is reassuring; that is a guarantee on your side, at least, of a dignified, honourable canvass."

"Oh, yes, sir," said Hickey.

He left gravely and scampered across the campus. Suddenly from the Woodhull Toots Cortell's trumpet squeaked out. At the same moment the first Anti-Fed banner was flung out, thus conceived:

TURN THE ROBBERS OUT
NO MORE GRAFTING
NO MORE GOUGING THE UNDER FORMERS
FACULTY SUPERVISION MEANS
SAVING TO THE POCKET
OUT WITH THE BLACKMAILERS

The astute and professional hand of the Honourable Crazy Opdyke was felt at once. The Anti-Fed party, while still advocating faculty control of the athletic finances for purposes of efficiency and economy, now shifted the ground by a series of brilliant strokes.

The third day of the campaign had hardly opened when the four fusion houses displayed prominently the following proclamation:

ECONOMY AND JIGGERS
FACULTY MANAGEMENT OF THE FINANCES
MEANS RIGID ECONOMY
PROTECTION OF THE WEAK
FROM THE TYRANNY OF THE TAX GATHERER
EQUITABLE PRO-RATA
LEVYING OF CONTRIBUTIONS
ECONOMY MEANS MORE JIGGERS
MORE JIGGERS MEANS
MORE HAPPINESS FOR THE GREATER NUMBER
VOTE FOR THE FATTER POCKETBOOK

Hardly had this argument to the universal appetite been posted before the Feds retorted by posting a proclamation:

FACULTY PLOT

EVIDENCE IS PILING UP THAT THE
PRESENT POLITICAL CAMPAIGN IS A
HUGE FACULTY CONSPIRACY TO DE-
PRIVE THE SCHOOL OF ITS LIBERTIES
BY UNDERGROUND DARK-LANTERN
METHODS, WHERE IT DOES NOT DARE
TO ATTEMPT IT OPENLY
THE APRON-STRINGS ARE IN POSSES-
SION OF A GIGANTIC CORRUPTION
FUND   WHO IS PUTTING UP?

When this attack became public the Anti-Feds were in deep deliberation, planning a descent on the Hamill House. The news of the outrageous charge was borne to the conference by Hungry Smeed, with tears in his eyes.

"Crazy," said Doc, "we must meet the charge, now, at once."

There was a chorus of assent.

"We will," said Crazy, diving into his pocket and producing a wad of paper. "This is what I've had up my sleeve from the beginning. This is the greatest state paper ever conceived."

"Let's have it," said Hickey, and Crazy proudly read:

THE FULL PROGRAMME

The Campaign of Slander and Villification Instituted by Tough McCarthy and His Myrmidons Will Not Deceive the Intelligent and Independent Voter. Anti-Federalist Candidates Only Are the Defendants of the Liberties of the School.

Anti-Fed. Candidates Stand Solemnly Pledged to Work For Increased Privileges.

ACCESS TO THE JIGGER-SHOP AT ALL TIMES
REMOVING THE LIMIT ON WEEKLY ALLOWANCES
ABOLITION OF THE HATEFUL COMPULSORY
BATH SYSTEM
BETTER FOOD   MORE FOOD
REGULATION OF SINKERS AND SCRAG-BIRDS
ESTABLISHMENT OF TWO SLEIGHING HOLIDAYS
CUSHIONED SEATS FOR CHAPEL

When this momentous declaration of principles was read there was an appalled silence, while Crazy, in the centre of the admiring circle, grew perceptibly.

Then a shriek burst out and Crazy was smothered in the arms of the regenerated Anti-Feds.

"Crazy will be President of the United States," said Turkey admiringly.

"Wonderful!"

"The bathroom plank will win us fifty votes."

"And what about the jigger vote?"

At this moment an egg passed rapidly through the open window and spread itself on the wall, while across the campus the figure of Mucker Reilly of the Kennedy was seen zigzagging for safety, with his thumb vulgarly applied to his nose.

The Executive Committee gazed at the wall, watching the yellow desecration gradually trickling into a map of South America.

"This means the end of argument," said Cheyenne sadly. "The campaign from now on will be bitter."

"If the appeal to force is going to be made," said Crazy, applying a towel, "we shall endeavour —Doc, shut the window—we shall endeavour to meet it."

"We have now a chance," said Egghead, brightening, "to prove that we are not Goo-Goos."

"Egghead, you are both intelligent and comforting," said Hickey. "The first thing is to corner the egg market."

"The Finance Committee," said Crazy wrathfully, "is empowered to buy, beg or borrow every egg, every squashy apple, every mushy tomato that can be detected and run down. From now on we shall wage a vigorous campaign."

The publication of the Anti-Fed programme roused the party cohorts to cheers and song. The panicky Feds strove desperately to turn the tide with the following warning:

HA! HA!

IT WON'T DO!

WE KNOW THE HAND!

Don't Be Deceived. Hickey is the Sheep in Wolf's Clothing. Stung to the Quick by Our Detection of the Criminal Alliance Between the Anti-Feds and the Faculty, Hickey, the King of the Goo-Goos, is Trying to Bleat Like a Wolf. It Won't Do! They Cannot Dodge the Issue. Stand Firm. Lawrenceville Must Not Be Made Into a Kindergarten.

But this could not stem the rising wave. The Hamill House turned its back on Federalism and threw in its lot with the foes of compulsory bath. Just before supper the Anti-Feds were roused to frenzy by the astounding news that the little Rouse House, isolated though it was from the rest of the school and under the very wing of the Davis, had declared Anti-Fed, for the love of combat that burned in its heroic band led by the redoubtable Charley De Soto and Scrapper Morrissey.

With the declaration of the different houses the first stage of the campaign ended. By supper every house was on a military footing and the dove of peace was hastening toward the horizon.

That night Mr. Baldwin waited in vain for the report of Hickey, waited and wondered. For the first time Baldwin, the enthusiast, began to be a little apprehensive of the forces he had unchained.

A little later Mr. Baronson chose to pay him a visit.

"Well, Baldwin, what news?" he said, drily. "Thoroughly satisfied with your new course in political education?"

"Why, the boys seem to take to it with enthusiasm," said Baldwin rather dubiously. "I think they're thoroughly interested."

"Interested? Yes—quite so. By the way, Baldwin," Baronson stopped a moment and scanned his young subordinate with pitying knowledge, "I'm going to retire for the night. If I had a cyclone cellar I'd move to it. I put you in charge of the house. If any attempt is made to set it on fire or dynamite it, go out and argue gently with the boys, and above all, impress upon them that they are the hope of the country and must set a standard. Reason with them, Baldwin, and above all, appeal to their better natures. Good-night."

Baldwin did not answer. He stood meditatively gazing out the window. From the Dickinson and the Kennedy magic lanterns were flashing campaign slogans on white sheets suspended at opposite houses. The uproar of cat-calls and hoots that accompanied the exhibitions left small reason to hope that they were couched in that clear, reasoning style which would uplift future American politics.

As he looked, from the Upper House the indignant and now thoroughly aroused fourth form started to parade with torch-lights and transparencies.

Presently the winding procession, clothed in super-
imposed night shirts, arrived with hideous clamour.
Dangling from a pole were two grotesque figures
stuffed with straw and decked with aprons; over-
head was the inscription, " Kings of the Goo-Goos,"
and one was labelled Hickey and one was labelled
Brother. Opposite his window they halted and
chanted in soft unison:

>Hush, hush, tread softly,
>Hush, hush, make no noise,
>Baldwin is the King of the Goo-Goos,
>Let him sleep,
>Let him sleep.

Shouted: LET HIM SLEEP!!!

Then the transparencies succeeded one another,
bobbing over the rolling current of indignant seniors.

>BACK TO THE KINDERGARTEN!
>WE WANT NO BROTHERLY LOVE!
>GOOD-BYE, BALDWIN! GOOD-BYE!

Baldwin drew down the shade and stepped from
the window. He heard a familiar step in the corridor, and quickly locked the door. Baronson
knocked; then he knocked again; after which he
moved away, chuckling.

When the fourth form procession arrived on its

tour around the circle the Dickinsonians were prepared to welcome it. Crazy Opdyke, head of the
literary bureau, stood by the lantern directing the
proclamations to be flashed on the sheet that hung
from the opposite house.

Hickey and Macnooder posted the orators at
strategic windows, supplying them with compressed
arguments in the form of eggs and soft apples.

" All ready? " said Opdyke as Hickey returned,
chuckling.

" Ready and willing," said Hickey.

" Here they come," said the Big Man.

" Is the Kennedy and the Woodhull with them? "
asked Hickey.

" Sure, they're trailing on behind," said Turkey.

A yell of defiance burst from the head of the procession as it reached the headquarters of the enemy.

" Start the literature," said Crazy.

Egghead, at the lantern, slipped in the first slides,
flashing them on the opposite sheet.

IT'S ALL OVER, BOYS

FEDERALISM IS IN THE SOUP

FEDERALISTS

THE UPPER HOUSE MYRMIDONS

THE DAVIS JAYHAWKERS

THE   WOODHULL   SORE   HEADS
THE   KENNEDY   MUCKERS
ANTI-FEDERALISTS
THE   ROUSE   INVINCIBLES
THE   CLEVE   INDEPENDENTS
THE   GRISWOLD   INTELLECTUALS
THE   GREEN   MUGWUMPS
THE   DICKINSON   SCHOLARS
THE   HAMILL   MISSIONARIES
GOOD-BYE,   FEDS!   GOOD-BYE!

"Now for a few personal references," said Crazy, smiling happily at the howls that greeted his first effort. "Egghead, shove them right along."

Another series was put forth:

WHY,   WOODHULL,   DID   WE   STEAL
YOUR   ICE   CREAM?
IS   TOUGH   McCARTHY'S   GANG   OF
BALLOT-STUFFERS   WITH   YOU?
WE   ARE   NOT   FOURTH-FORM   PUPPY
DOGS
HELLO,   TOUGH,   HOW   DOES   IT   FEEL   TO
BE   A   PUPPY   DOG?

"What are they shouting now?" said Hickey, peering over at the turbulent chaos below.

"They are re-questing us to come out!" said the Egghead.

The night was filled with the shrieks of the helpless Feds.

"Come out!"

" We dare you to come out! "

" Come out, you Dickinson Goo-Goos."

" Why, they're really getting excited," said
Hickey. " They're hopping right up and down."

" We will give them a declaration of principles,"
said Crazy. " Egghead, give them the principles;
Hickey, notify the orators to prepare the compressed
arguments. The word is ' BIFF.' "

Hickey went tumbling upstairs; the Egghead delivered the new series.

WHY, FEDS, DON'T GET PEEVISH
THIS IS AN ORDERLY CAMPAIGN
A QUIET, ORDERLY CAMPAIGN
REMEMBER, WE MUST UPLIFT THE
NATION

Outside, the chorus of hoots and cat-calls gave way
to a steady rhythmic chant:

GOO-GOOS, GOO-GOOS, GOO-GOOS!

" How unjust! " said Crazy, sadly. " We must
clear ourselves; we must nail the lie—in a quiet,
orderly way! Let her go, Egghead; Cheyenne, give
Hickey the cue."

On the sheet suddenly flashed out:

WE ARE GOO-GOOS, ARE WE? BIFF!

At the same moment, from a dozen windows descended a terrific broadside of middle-aged eggs, assorted vegetables and squashy fruit.

The Federalist forces, utterly off their guard, dripping with egg and tomato, vanished like a heap of leaves before a whirlwind, while from the Anti-Federalist houses exultant shrieks of victory burst forth.

"If we are to be called Goo-Goos," said Crazy, proudly, "we have, at least, made Goo-Goo a term of honour."

"To-morrow should be a very critical day in the campaign," said Macnooder, pensively.

"I suggest that on account of the uncertain state of the weather," said Hickey, wisely, "that all window-blinds should be closed and locked."

"I think," said Cheyenne, "that we had better march to chapel in close formation."

"Are there any more arguments left?" said Crazy.

"Quite a number."

"They must be delivered to-night," said Crazy, firmly. "No egg shall be allowed to spoil—in this house."

At eleven o'clock that night, as the head master sat

in his room in distant Boston, giving the last touches to the address which he had prepared for the following day on the " Experiment of Self-Government and Increased Individual Responsibility in Primary Education," the following telegram was handed to him:

> Come back instantly. School in state of anarchy. Rioting and pillaging unchecked. Another day may be too late. Baldwin's course in political education.
>
> BARONSON.

When the Doctor, after a night's precipitous travel, drove on to the campus he had left picturesque and peaceful but a few days before, he could hardly believe his eyes. The circle of houses was stained and spotted with the marks of hundreds of eggs and the softer vegetables. From almost every upper window a banner (often ripped to shreds) or a mutilated proclamation was displayed. Proclamations blossomed on every tree, couched in vitriolic language. Two large groups of embattled boys, bearing strange banners, were converging across the campus, with haggard, hysterical faces, fists clenched and muscles strung in nervous tension, waiting the shock of the approaching clash.

The Doctor sprang from the buggy and advanced toward chapel with determined, angry strides. At the sight of the familiar figure a swift change went over the two armies, on the point of flying at each other's throats. The most bloodthirsty suddenly quailed, the most martial scowls gave place to looks of innocence. In the twinkling of an eye every banner had disappeared, and the two armies, breaking formation, went meekly and fearfully into chapel.

The Doctor from his rostrum looked down upon the school. Under his fierce examination every glance fell to the hymn-book.

"Young gentlemen of the Lawrenceville School, I will say just one word," began the head master. "This political campaign will STOP, NOW, *AT ONCE!*" He paused at the spectacle of row on row of blooming eyes and gory features, and, despite himself, his lips twitched.

In an instant the first ranks began to titter, then a roar of laughter went up from the pent-up, hysterical boys. They laughed until they sobbed, for the first time aware of the ridiculousness of the situation. Then as the Doctor, wisely refraining from further discourse, dismissed them, they swayed out on the campus where the Davis fell into the arms of the

Dickinson, and Fed and Anti-Fed rolled with laughter on the ground.

When Hickey, that afternoon, brazenly sought out Mr. Baldwin, a certain staccato note in the greeting caused a dozen careful phrases to die on his tongue.

"Don't hesitate, Hicks," said Baldwin, smiling. coldly.

"I came, sir," said Hicks, looking down, "I came —that is, I—Mr. Baldwin, sir, I'm sorry it turned out such a failure."

"Of course, Hicks," said Baldwin, softly, "of course. It must be a great disappointment—to you. But it is not a failure, Hicks. On the contrary, it has been a great success—this campaign of education. I have learned greatly. By the way, Hicks, kindly announce to the class that I shall change my method of hearing recitations. I have a new system —based on the latest discoveries in the laws of probability. Announce also an examination for to-morrow."

"To-morrow?" said Hickey, astounded.

"On the review—in the interest of education—my education. Don't look down, Hicks—I cherish no resentment against you—none at all."

"Against me?" said Hickey, aggrieved.

" My feelings are of gratitude and affection only. You have been the teacher and I the scholar—— but——" He paused and surveyed the persecuted Hicks with the smile of the anaconda for the canary, " but, Hicks, my boy, whatever else may be the *indifference* of the masters toward your education, when you leave Lawrenceville you will not be weak in——mathematics."

THE MARTYRDOM OF WILLIAM HICKS

Hickey had now reached the height of his fame. Intoxicated by success, he forgot all prudence, or rather his revolt became an appetite that demanded constant feeding. He no longer concealed his past exploits, he even went so far as to announce the escapades he planned.

"You are running your head into the noose, Hickey, my boy," said Macnooder, sadly; "every master in the school has got his eye on you."

"I know it," said Hickey proudly, "but they've got to catch me."

"Your position is different," objected Macnooder, "now you are suspected. And do you want me to tell you the truth? Your trick about the clappers was too clever. If you could imagine that, you were at the bottom of other things. That's what the Doctor will say to himself when he thinks it over."

"The Doctor plays square," retorted Hickey; "he won't do anything on suspicion. Let him try and catch me, let them all try. If they get me fair and square, I'll take my punishment. I say, Doc, just you wait. I've got something up my sleeve that'll make them all sit up."

"Good Lord!" said the Egghead, who was of the party, "you don't mean you're going on?"

"Egghead," said Hickey, impressively, "I've made up my mind that I just can't live without doing one thing more!"

"Heavens, Hickey! what now?"

"I've got a craving, Egghead, to sleep in Tabby's bed."

"No!"

"Fact."

"What do you mean?"

" Just that. I intend to sleep, not just pop in and out, to *sleep* two hours in Tabby's nice, white, little bed."

" Gee whiz, Hickey! When? "

" Some night that's coming pretty soon."

" When Tabby's away——"

" No, sir, when Tabby's here—after Tabby himself has been in it. After that I'm going to get back at Big Brother."

" You're crazy! "

" I'm backing my feelings."

" You'll bet on it? "

" As much as you want."

The scornful Egghead, thus provoked, offered ten to one against him. Hickey accepted at once.

During the day the news spread and the bets came flying in. As to his plans, Hickey preserved a cloaked mystery, promising only that the feat should take place within the fortnight.

Each night toward midnight, he slipped out of Sawtelle's window (Sawtelle being sworn to deadly secrecy). He remained out an hour, sometimes two, and came back sleepy and chuckling. About this time the report began to spread that burglars were in the vicinity.

The Gutter Pup, who roomed on the first floor of the Woodhull, took a solemn oath that having been waked up by a strange scratching noise at his window, he had seen four masked figures with bull's-eye lanterns scurrying away. The next report came from Davis with added picturesqueness. The school became wrought up to an extraordinary pitch of excitement in which even the masters joined after a period of incredulity.

When the proper stage of frenzy arrived, Hickey took into his confidence a dozen allies.

At exactly two o'clock on a moonless night, Beauty Sawtelle, waiting, watch in hand, gave a horrid shriek and sent a baseball bat crashing through his window, where he afterward swore four masked faces had glared in on him. At the same time the Egghead raised his window and emptied a revolver into the air, shouting:

"Thieves, thieves, there they go!"

Immediately every waiting boy sprang out of bed armed with revolvers, shot-guns, brickbats, Japanese swords and what not, and rushed downstairs, shouting:

"Stop thief!"

Mr. Tapping, startled from his slumbers by the

uproar, seized a bird-gun and, guided by Hungry Smeed and the Red Dog, rushed out of doors and valorously took the lead of the searching party. By this time the racket had spread about the campus and boys in flimsy garments, ludicrously armed, came pouring out the other houses and joined the wild hunt for the masked marauders. Suddenly, from the direction of Foundation House, a series of shots exploded amid yells of excitement. At once the mass that had been churning in the middle of the campus, set off with a rush. The cry went up that the burglars had been discovered and were fleeing down the road to Trenton. Five minutes later the campus was silent, as boys and masters swept along the highway, their cries growing fainter in the distance.

Meanwhile, Hickey had not lost a second. Hardly had Mr. Tapping's pink pajamas rushed from the Dickinson, when Hickey, entering the study, locked the door and set to work. In a jiffy he had the mattress and bedclothes out the window, down into the waiting hands of Macnooder and the Egghead, who piled them on a ready wheelbarrow. In less than five minutes the iron bedstead, separated into its four component parts, followed. The whole, packed on the wheelbarrow, was hastily rushed into the darkness by the rollicking three. According to the plan, Hickey directed them past Memorial and into the baseball cage, where, by the light of the indispensable dark-lantern, they put the bed together, placed on it the bedding, and saw Hickey crawl blissfully under cover.

When Mr. Tapping returned after an hour's fruitless pursuit down the dusty road, it had begun to dawn upon him, in common with other athletic members of the faculty, that he had been hoaxed. Mr. Tapping was very sensitive to his dignity, and dignity was exceedingly difficult in pajamas, in the chill of a night with a ridiculous bird-gun over his shoulder and an assorted lot of semi-bare savages chuckling about him. Tired, covered with dust, and sheepish, he returned to the Dickinson, gave orders for every one to return to his room and wearily toiled up to seek his comfortable bed.

The vacancy that greeted his eyes left him absolutely incredulous, then beside himself with rage. If on that moment he could have laid his hands on Hickey, he would have done him bodily injury. That Hickey was the perpetrator of this new outrage, as of the previous ones, he never for a moment doubted. His instinct needed no proofs, and in such enmities the instinct is strong. He went directly to Hickey's room, finding it, as he had expected, empty. He sat there half an hour, an hour, fruitlessly. Then he made the rounds of the house and returned to the room, seated himself, folded his arms violently, set his teeth and prepared to wait. He heard four o'clock strike, then five, and he began to nod. He rose, shook himself, returned to his seat and presently fell asleep, and in this condition Hickey, returning, found him.

The bell rang six, and Mr. Tapping, starting up guiltily, glanced hastily at the bed and assured himself thankfully that it was empty. Moreover, conclusive evidence, the counterpane had not been turned down, so Hickey had not gone to bed at all.

By prodigies of will power he remained awake, consoled by the fact that he held at last the evidence needed to debarrass himself of his tormentor. At seven o'clock the gym bell rang the rising hour. Mr. Tapping rose triumphant. Suddenly he stopped and looked down in horror. Something had moved under the bed. The next moment

Hickey's face appeared under the skirts of the trailing bedspread—Hickey's face, a mirror of sleepy amazement, as he innocently asked:

"Why, Mr. Tapping, what *is* the matter?"

"Hicks!" exclaimed Mr. Tapping, too astounded to gather his thoughts, "is that you, Hicks?"

"Yes, sir."

"What are you doing under there?"

"Please sir," said Hickey, "I'm troubled with insomnia and sometimes this is the only way I can sleep."

At two o'clock Hickey was a second time summoned to Foundation House. He went in perfect faith. Nothing had miscarried, there was not the slightest evidence against him. If he was questioned he would refuse to answer—that was all. It had been a morning of exquisite triumph for him. Tabby's bed had not been discovered until ten o'clock, and the transferal to the Dickinson, made in full daylight, had been witnessed by the assembled school. He went across the campus, light of feet and proud of heart, aware of the scores of discreetly admiring eyes that followed him, hearing pleasantly the murmurs which buzzed after him:

" Oh, you prodigious Hickey—oh, you daredevil! "

Of course, the Doctor would be in a towering rage. Hickey was not unreasonable, he understood and expected a natural exhibition of vexation. What could the Doctor do, after all? Ask him questions which he would refuse to answer—that was all, but that was not evidence.

He found the Doctor alone, quietly writing at his desk, and received a smile and an invitation to be seated. Somehow the tranquillity of the head master's attitude did not reassure Hickey. He would have preferred a little more agitation, but this satisfied calm was disquieting.

He stood with his hands behind his back, twirling his cap, studying the photographs of Grecian architecture on the walls, finding it awfully still and wishing the Doctor would begin.

Presently the Doctor turned, put down his spectacles, shoved back from the desk and glanced at Hickey with a smile, saying:

" Well, Hicks, we're going to let you go."

" Beg your pardon, sir," said Hickey, smiling frankly back, " you said——"

" We're going to let you take a vacation."

" Me? "

" You."

Hickey stood a long moment, open-mouthed, staring.

" Do you mean to say," he said, at last, with an effort, " that I am expelled? "

" Not expelled," said the Doctor, suavely, " we don't like that word; we're going to let you go, that's all."

" For what reason? " said Hickey, defiantly.

" For no reason at all," answered the Doctor, smoothly. " There is no reason, there can be no reason, Hicks. We're just naturally going to make up our minds to part with you. You see, Hicks," he continued, tilting back and gazing reminiscently at the ceiling, " we've had a rather agitated session here, rather extraordinary. The trouble seems to have broken out in the Dickinson about the time of the little surprise party at which Mr. Tapping did not assist! Then a few days later our chapel service was disturbed and our janitor put to considerable trouble; next the school routine was thrown into confusion by the removal of the clapper. We passed a very disagreeable period—much confusion, very little study, and the nerves of the faculty were thrown into such a state that even you, Hicks, were sus-

" ' He hadn't any proof,' he said, brokenly, ' no proof—damn him ! ' "

" ' Nothing but a " suveneer," gents, nothing
guaranteed ' "   (Page 123)

pected. Then there was the political campaign, a
subject too painful to analyse. Last night we lost
a great deal of sleep—and sleep is most necessary
to the growing boy. All these events have followed
with great regularity, and while they have not lacked
in picturesqueness, we have, we fear, been forgetting the main object of our life here—to study a
little."

" Doctor, I——" broke in Hickey.

" No, Hicks, you misunderstand me," said the Doctor, reproachfully. " All this is true, but that is *not*
why we are going to let you go. We are going to
let you go, Hicks, for a much more conscientious
reason; we're parting with you, Hicks, because we
feel we no longer have anything to teach you."

" Doctor, I'd like to know," began Hickey, with
a great lump in his throat. Then he stopped and
looked at the floor. He knew his hour had sounded.

" Hicks, we part in sorrow," said the Doctor,
" but we have the greatest faith in your career. We
expect in a few years to claim you as one of our
foremost alumni. Perhaps some day you will give
us a library which we will name after you. No, don't
be disheartened. We have the greatest admiration
for your talents, admiration and respect. Anyone

who can persuade two hundred and fifty keen-eyed Lawrenceville boys to pay one dollar apiece for silver gilt scrap-iron souvenirs worth eleven cents apiece because they may or may not be genuine bits of a stolen clapper—anyone who can do that is needed in the commercial development of our country."

"Doctor, do you—do you call this justice?" said Hickey, with tears in his voice.

"No," said the Doctor, frankly, "I call it a display of force. You see, Hicks, you've beaten us at every point, and so all we can do is to let you go."

"I'll hire a lawyer," said Hicks, brokenly.

"I thought you would," said the Doctor, "only I hope you will be easy on us, Hicks, for we haven't much money for damage suits."

"Then I'm to be fired," said Hickey, forcing back the tears, "fired just for nothing!"

"Just for nothing, Hicks," assented the Doctor, rising to close the painful interview, "and, Hicks, as one last favour, we would like to request that it be by the evening train. We have lost a great deal of sleep lately."

"Just for nothing," repeated Hickey, hoarsely.

"Just for nothing," replied the Doctor, as he closed the door.

At six o'clock, in the midst of indignant hundreds, Hickey climbed to the top of the stage, where his trunks had already been deposited. Nothing could comfort him, neither the roaring cheers that echoed again and again to his name, nor the hundreds of silent hand-shakes or muttered vows to continue the good fight. His spirit was broken. All was dark before him. Neither right nor justice existed in the world.

Egghead and Macnooder, visibly affected, reached up for the last hand-shakes.

"Keep a stiff upper lip, old man," said the Egghead.

"Don't you worry, Hickey, old boy," said Macnooder; "we'll attend to Tabby."

Then Hickey, bitterly, from the caverns of his heart, spoke, raising his fist toward Tabby's study window.

"He hadn't any proof," he said, brokenly, "no proof—damn him!"

Vlba

5 p. 10

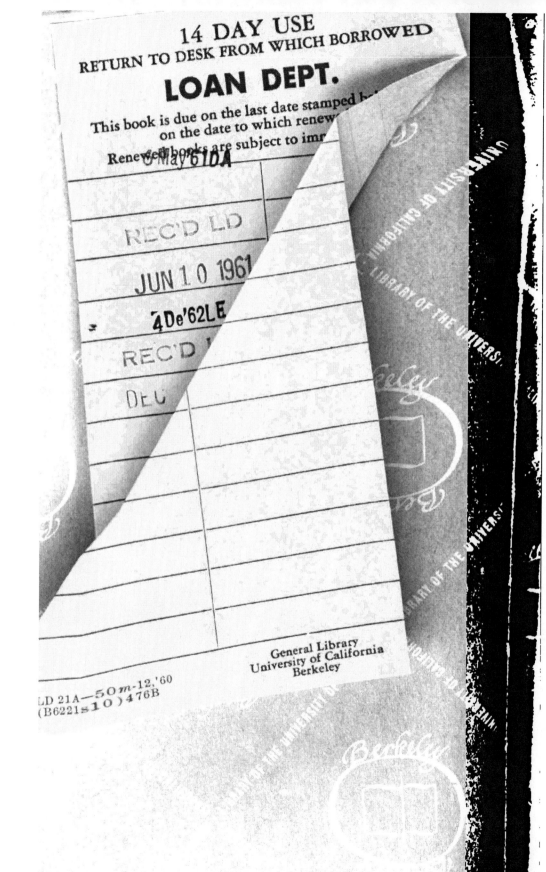

LaVergne, TN USA
09 June 2010
185571LV00003B/100/P